How to Craft a J Cozy Mystery

An Intensive Guide to
Traditional Murder Mysteries
& Writing the Modern Whodunit
by Andrea J. Johnson

Guidebooks for Success

WRITER PRODUCTIVITY SERIES - BOOK 1

ISBN: 978-1-7376880-1-3

1. Detective and mystery stories—Technique. 2. Fiction Technique. 3. Authorship

To receive a monthly email newsletter full of free writing advice and updates about future Writer Productivity Series books, register at https://ajthenovelist.com/sign-up/

About the Author

Andrea J. Johnson is a writer and editor whose expertise lies in traditional mysteries and romance. She holds a B.A. in English from Swarthmore College, an M.F.A. in Writing Popular Fiction from Seton Hill University, and a copyediting certification from UC San Diego. Her craft essays have appeared on several websites such as *CrimeReads*, *Litreactor*, *DIY MFA*, *Submittable*, and *Funds for Writers*. She has also written for the women's lifestyle websites *Popsugar* and *The List Daily*. Andrea's novels include the cozy courtroom whodunit series the Victoria Justice Mysteries, whose stories focus on a trial stenographer turned amateur sleuth (think *Murder, She Wrote* meets *The Pelican Brief*). When she isn't researching or writing mysteries, you can find her helping novice writers develop their steamy contemporary romances.

Books by Andrea J. Johnson

Victoria Justice Mystery Series:
Poetic Justice
Deceptive Justice

Dedication

To Jacqueline, you are loved more than you know.

CONTENTS

INTRODUCTION

Cozy mysteries have earned steady popularity in the contemporary fiction market because of the familiarity promised by the closed communal setting. In a cozy, the themes are universal and the main character is someone relatable like the upbeat girl next door or the savvy grandmother—both of whom rely on their friends and family to help solve the crime.

This is a pleasant contrast to detective stories or crime novels that saddle the reader with an inscrutable, ill-tempered sleuth, who toils under his own deductions and barely allows the audience to play along in solving the crime. That's not said to bash other mystery subgenres. Rather, the statement is meant to highlight the idea that relationships are an essential part of what make cozies...well, cozy...and popular among readers looking for a safe wholesome escape where justice prevails.

We'll talk more about the popularity of cozies and their history in the opening chapter, but let's first outline exactly what this book has to offer and what I hope you'll learn.

This guide assumes you know the basics of narrative storytelling and how to infuse emotion into your fiction, so we will only touch on those concepts briefly. If you want additional help in the aforementioned areas, purchase copies of *Scene and Structure* by Jack M. Bickham and *The Emotional Craft of Fiction* by Donald Maass.

My main focus will be on the genre expectations and rules for writing a cozy mystery such as building a memorable community and crafting clever clues. Please review the table of contents for a more granular description of the topics covered. But generally speaking, this work will shine a light on the common questions about crafting a whodunit:

> What is the difference between cozies and other mystery fiction?

> Why it is so important that cozies play fair with the audience, and how do I do it?

> What are the elements of the cozy mystery plot?

> What should I have in place before tackling my first draft?

Please note this text will focus on what it takes to write a full-length mystery novel. Even though you will able to use most of this advice for novellas or short fiction, that is not our focus. With that in mind, here is a clear list of what this guide will not offer:

> A marketing or submission plan
> Advice on obtaining an agent or securing a book deal
> Advice on writing a series
> Advice on self-publishing
> A rigid way of doing things

The last point is important. While I want to give you a solid foundation for what goes into a killer cozy, the manner in which you go about this task should mesh with your skill and sensibilities. I am not here to dissuade anyone from doing something that has brought them positive results. I am, however, interested in making sure your mysteries contain the necessary ingredients to get fans addicted to your work.

Therefore, this book is for anyone who is new to the genre and needs a push getting started. You will receive a detailed roadmap that will help turn an idea into a work of art. You can read this guide in sections or from beginning to end, but I encourage you to take notes in your own hand so that the concepts get into your bones. Most chapters contain recaps or grow tips so that you can easily refer back to the different sections for a quick answer about a specific topic. You should also bookmark the glossary in the back in case there are terms that are unfamiliar. But most importantly, follow up on any supplemental material mentioned, particularly if it covers one of your weak spots.

As alluded to earlier, cozy mysteries have a specific structure that fans expect authors to follow. This construct is not impossible to learn on one's own, but it is perilous. If this is the genre you've chosen for your career, I encourage you to embrace the concept of life-long learning because fiction, like any other art, has tricky nuances that are always changing.

During my writer's journey, I took this advice to the extreme by attending graduate school for an MFA in Writing Popular Fiction. Of course, you don't have to go to such lengths (unless you want to!), especially when I've already done the work for you.

So with career growth as our mindset, consider this book my way of sharing what I've learned while getting you excited about your own projects and saving you a little time and money along the way. Whether you're a plotter or a pantser, my goal is for you to become passionate about taking your writing to the next level while giving you the tools to craft the perfect mystery.

In essence, you'll leave this book knowing exactly what elements will make your cozy...a killer!

MYSTERY HISTORY

According to Malice Domestic[1], a national organization of fans and writers committed to the mystery genre, a cozy whodunit "contains no explicit sex, excessive gore, or gratuitous violence, and takes place in a confined setting containing characters who know one another." Modern writers might also add that the death of children or animals is a no-go in this subgenre as are long-standing or permanent injuries to the core cast of characters. The books should be clean enough for a 12-year-old, but interesting enough for a mature woman of 55 years or older as that's the audience demographic for a cozy[2].

Historically, these mysteries find their roots in the decades between the First and Second World Wars (1914-1945), a period notably known as the Golden Age of Detective Fiction, where plots centered on intellectual puzzles and deductive reasoning. American writer Edgar Allan Poe's short story "The Murders in the Rue Morgue" (1841) is often cited as the work first noted for using detection methods. This was later followed by English author Wilkie Collins, who is typically credited as the author of the first official mystery novel, *The Woman in White* (1860). And yet, it wasn't until 1887 when Arthur Conan Doyle first published *A Study in Scarlet* and introduced Sherlock Holmes that the genre came alive. Soon thereafter, the Golden Age flourished bringing us esteemed British mystery novelists such as Ronald Knox, Agatha Christie, Dorothy L. Sayers, Phillip MacDonald, and Patricia Wentworth.

---

1. https://www.malicedomestic.org/

2. https://thoughtcatalog.com/porter-anderson/2015/01/taking-a-deep-dive-into-mystery-with-nielsen-murder-she-read/

After World War II, the genre gained solid footing in the United States, where novels like Dashiell Hammett's *Maltese Falcon* (1930) and Raymond Chandler's *The Big Sleep* (1939) explored the grittier side of detection with tough private eyes, and Erle Stanley Gardner added a few legal thrills to the genre by introducing his Perry Mason character in *The Case of the Velvet Claws* (1933).

However, the term "cozies" wasn't fully embraced as the name for the subgenre until the late 20th century as modern writers began to recreate the work of the Golden Age. The contemporary cozy includes an amateur sleuth whose profession aids in the solution of the crime, thereby giving the audience a level of plot accessibility not available with a technique-driven detective at the helm—such as Arthur Conan Doyle's Sherlock Holmes or Agatha Christie's Hercule Poirot.

This open communication between author, reader, and gumshoe gives the cozy audience an opportunity to solve the crime alongside the investigator. Modern cozy series like my own, Victoria Justice Mysteries, adhere to the classic mystery structure of the Golden Age while expanding upon the genre by integrating aspects of the sleuth's career and personality into the overall detection and resolution of the crime.

So let's first outline the main elements of a cozy mystery. Most cozies are set in a small town, but this is not a requirement as long as the setting is somewhat secluded or sets a tone of community and shared values. This could be the suburban appeal of a retired cop turned pet sitter such as Blaize Clement's Dixie Hemingway Mystery series or the insular nature of a specific group within a big city as with Julie Hyzy's White House Chef Mystery novels. My own series mainly takes place in the courtroom of a rural town, but a national baking contest, a Hollywood movie set, or a dinner party will do if a suitable microcosm is not available. When everyone has a communal connection, the sleuthing becomes easier for the amateur detective, and the suspect list remains visible to the audience at all times. Thus, the gumshoe—often female due to the subgenre's largely female readership—relies on her friends,

family, and enemies to inform her crime solving. She may also have a relationship with the victim, good or bad, that motivates her to take the
case and informs her methods of detection.

In other detective fiction subgenres—hard-boiled, police procedurals, thrillers—the reader or investigator may know the identity of the
killer upfront, so the focus becomes *can they catch the culprit before it
is too late*? In a cozy, the sleuth may interact with the killer, but the
murderer's identity does not surface until the end. Humor also plays a
role by acting as a counterbalance to the mayhem although most cozies
avoid depicting serious bloodshed. It helps that the killers in these stories aren't sociopaths or ne'er-do-wells. Instead, they are rational and articulate. During the story, they hide in plain sight and interact with the
protagonist in a relatively normal manner, and this camaraderie with
the investigator inevitably leads to them explaining their motives upon
capture—usually personal motives that connect with the community's
culture.

Of course, all great fiction is fueled by conflict, or the concept that
one entity stands in the way of what the other wants. In cozy mysteries,
since the stories are built in such an idyllic world, the conflict strikes a
stark contrast that can be boiled down to the idea of good versus evil.
That's why the main conflict is typically murder since it provides the
most dramatic struggle with the highest stakes—life versus death. Yet,
the key to a good cozy is that along with the crime and the detection,
the narrative promises a return to the ideal world. Along the way, you
may develop themes around karma or retribution, share recipes, or develop kooky characters who will carry from book to book, but the murder and the restoration of justice are the baseline you must return to
throughout the novel.

In addition, the cozy mystery puzzle creates a competition of "who
will triumph first" between the reader and sleuth—and to a degree the
villain, whose efforts should appear to succeed at first even though the
readers' expectations require he be thwarted in the end. Smart writers

will even use their crime to raise social, political, or psychological issues in the community like James Grippando's Jack Swyteck Series. The choice of who dies can also say something as well. For example, does the murder of the mayor create outrage, or is the moneygrubbing politician getting what's coming to him? What does the community reaction say about the world in which the story is set? How does the death alter society for the better or worse? Questions like these will help fuel the story and shape the conclusion.

Recap: Mystery History

Cozies are lighthearted mysteries focused on a domestic crime with a limited suspect pool and a villain whose reasons for murder pertain to personal relationships. Below you will find the key reader expectations for the subgenre. These are essential ingredients that if left out, may result in an entirely different product—one that perhaps reads more like private detective fiction or a thriller. Of course, as with anything, there are always exceptions to the rules and even Dame Agatha Christie bent, broke, and modified some them to suit a particular novel's needs. So if you must absolutely rebel against the common conventions, do so knowingly and with good purpose. However, I absolutely urge anyone new to cozies to stick with this list.

> Amateur sleuth (usually female)

> Entertaining or knowledgeable sidekick

> Ineffective law enforcement

> Light in tone or humorous[1]

> Bloodless off-stage crime

> Despicable victim[2]

> No profanity, explicit sex, or gory violence

> Vivid setting in a small town, closed community, or tight professional circle

> A web of friends and family the sleuth relies as sounding board or for information

> Profession that steers detection

> Fair play puzzle

> Active detection by the amateur sleuth

> Justice restored with the criminals getting unmasked and punished or exiled

[1] Many cozies rely on character- or situation-driven humor. This means the laughs derive from the protagonist's idiosyncrasies (e.g. *Monk* and his OCD) or the protagonist getting himself into a wacky situation (e.g. Shawn Spencer on *Psych*) rather than the writer crafting witty banter or having laugh-out-loud jokes (e.g. *Veronica Mars* and *Buffy the Vampire Slayer*), so don't feel intimidated if you're uncomfortable writing humor. Also, be aware that the crazier the humor, the less seriously the audience will take the characters' interactions and the mystery's solution. You don't want to give the reader the impression a person's death lacks consequence, so look for moments of gravity. On the flip side, if you're looking to write a story grounded in realism or have some darker elements, feel free to relegate your comedic elements to the background until levity is needed. Just keep in mind that at the very least, the narrative should end on an upbeat note.

[2]We didn't cover the concept of a despicable victim in the main text because this practice is less common in the modern cozy. However, the victim in a traditional mystery is often someone who is hated, envied, or morally bankrupt. During the Golden Age, it was a tacit rule that the victim was a person the fictional community found deplorable—and by extension, someone the audience would dislike—so the reader could remain focused on the puzzle. Earl F. Bargainnier, author of *The Gentle Art of Murder: The Detective Fiction of Agatha Christie* (1980), explains this convention in practical terms: "If the victim is so objectionable that everyone has a motive, not only does this intensify the mystery, but it also frees the reader from any sense of guilt in accepting the death calmly." However, I would argue that this trope has grown predictable over the years in the same manner as has a solution that decrees: *The butler did it!* To always rely on a despicable victim means audiences can spot who will die from the first few paragraphs, leaving the potential for added suspense (i.e. who will die first?) untapped. Ideally, even the murder itself should have a small element of surprise that gives the audience a fun little gasp: *Oh, my goodness. I can't believe they just killed Colonel Mustard.* But of course, how you choose to handle this is up to you.

Fair Play

For a cozy to be truly satisfying, the plot must adhere to the rules of fair play. According to *The Golden Age of Murder* by Martin Edwards, these rules were published in 1929 when British mystery writer Ronald Knox introduced *The Best [English] Detective Stories of the Year* anthology with what he called a "Decalogue" or the "Ten Commandments of Detection." Later adopted by the London Detective Club[1]—a group of British mystery writers that included such greats as Agatha Christie and Dorothy L. Sayers—these rules aided the audience's ability to play along with the sleuth and shaped a growing genre.

Some of Knox's rules included things like encouraging the writer, especially when using a sidekick to narrate the action, to avoid concealing any thoughts, insights, or points of detection from the audience. Here are a few of the other prominent rules as listed in his essay: "The criminal must be someone mentioned in the early part of the story . . . . No accident must ever help the detective . . . . The detective must not himself commit the crime . . . . The detective must not light on any clues that are not instantly produced for the inspection of the reader."

Fair play allows the audience to become an active participant in the story. Thanks to these rules, fans of the genre not only benefit from the emotional highs and lows of the plot, but the thrill of victory and the agony of defeat that comes with getting the puzzle right or wrong.

The level of engagement possible in these stories mimic the passions, tension, and suspense of our daily lives. And the career-based theme often associated with cozies—knitters, bakers, hair dressers—helps to expand upon Knox's fair play rules because it gives the audience a context in which to piece together their puzzle. For example, the lead character in the Victoria Justice Mysteries is a trial stenographer, so the audience knows she will only be able to view and analyze the clues within the context of her acute skills of observation, organization, concentration, and attentiveness as a stenotypist. Of course, cozies require a certain suspension of disbelief with regard to how much the amateur detective's profession or skill can assist with crime detection. However, this discrepancy plays into the audience's unspoken desire that the ordinary person can rise to the challenge of an extraordinary situation and opens the door for the reader to solve the crime alongside the sleuth.

By melding the rules of fair play with the professional skills of the protagonist, the audience feels a sense of surety that a solution is nigh even if they have not been able to follow each one of the author's clues and red herrings. This surety leads to a calming effect that permits the audience to turn a portion of their concern to the character's plight rather than worry over the complexities of the mystery plot. Granted, the reader should still be pleased when the murderer's identity unfolds. The author wants the audience to exclaim, *I suspected as much,* or gasp, *I didn't expect that, but it makes perfect sense in retrospect.* To surprise without breaking the rules of fair play is to achieve mastery within the genre.

Cozy authors achieve this mastery by giving their protagonists a moral compass that is stronger than the average. Justice must prevail. Unlike hard-boiled detective tales or thrillers, cozy endings leave no room for ethical ambiguity.

Cozies further capitalize on the fair play rules and the classic mystery structure by ramping up characterization. The players in each story should pop off the page in a manner that ensures readers care about their personality and storylines long after the novel ends. That's one of the reasons why the sleuths in cozies are amateurs. The protagonist becomes a part of the investigation because they work with, care for, or share DNA with the parties involved in the crime, which feeds into the motivation of the entire cast. On the other hand, a professional gumshoe's detachment from the overall scenario places the spotlight more on the procedure of detection.

However, do not mistake a detective's amateur status as a writer's opportunity to dilute the plot. View this status as the author's opportunity to personalize the protagonist. By developing stories that make fewer demands on the sleuth's methods of detection, authors can create a main character whose story arc includes life lessons like love and loss. This humanizing aspect appeals to cozy fans who might not remember one plot from another but will recall the overall theme.

For example, the challenge for the protagonist in my Victoria Justice series is learning to stand up for herself, and this lesson becomes apparent in every relationship. Most notably, when she befriends a disgraced local cop to aid in her detection. In most cozies, she'd fall head over heels in love with him, but since she can't fully trust him, she never allows herself to become the clichéd damsel in distress. Her guarded approach saves her from duplicity but also provides a notable moral dilemma readers can debate as Victoria's life continues in future novels.

[1]The London Detection Club was founded in 1928 by Anthony Berkeley as a way of upholding the elevated professional standards held by its most prominent members—some of whom included S.S. Van Dine, Agatha Christie, Dorothy L. Sayers, H.C. Bailey, and John Dickson Carr. In fact, this commitment to crime writing excellence was evident—or should I say "is evident" as the organization still exists although in a less prominent form—in the oath taken by newly initiated members. Part of which reads as follows:

> "Do you promise that your detectives shall well and truly detect the crimes presented to them, using those wits which it may please you to bestow upon them and not placing reliance on nor making use of divine revelation, feminine intuition, mumbo-jumbo, jiggery-pokery, coincidence, or the act of God? Do you solemnly swear never to conceal a vital clue from the reader? Do you promise to observe a seemly moderation in the use of gangs, conspiracies, death-rays, ghost, hypnotism, trapdoors, super-criminals and lunatics; and utterly and forever to foreswear mysterious poisons unknown to science?"

As for our modern adherence to this last question, unless your book intentionally contains elements that fall into the paranormal subgenre, there shouldn't be an unforeshadowed magical or mystical event that solves the crime, acts as a deus ex machina, or provides a catchall solution to an otherwise impossible situation. To avoid this potential pitfall, make sure the rules for your supernatural world are clearly defined and the boundaries for the magic or mysticism used are apparent to the audience before incorporating those elements into your crime narrative. For a great example of how to do it right, see Alexia Gordon's Gethsemane Brown Mystery series.

Recap: Fair Play

In lieu of a more succinct summary, let me introduce you to S.S. Van Dine, an American novelist of the Golden Age, whose "Twenty Rules for Writing Detective Stories" essay helped shape the way we write cozies today. First published in the September 1928 issue of *American Magazine* and reprinted in the omnibus *Philo Vance Murder Cases* (1936), his rules are similar to Knox's and are also considered part of the foundational definition of "playing fair" with the reader. I won't transcribe all twenty here since some like the no love interest and the no secret society rules have become outdated. Yet, the majority still pertain to the modern cozy with regard to creating a puzzle in which the audience can take part. Below, you will find my summation of his most pertinent rules.

> Readers must have an equal opportunity to solve the case alongside the detective. Therefore, all clues must be open, apparent, and clearly described.

> Readers cannot be tricked or deceived other than those legitimately played by the criminal against the detective.

> The sleuth cannot be the culprit.

> The sleuth must be proactive and engage in active detection.

> The sleuth may have multiple sources of help or a sidekick, but there should be one main detective to avoid a disjointed and unfollowable thread of logic for the audience.

> The killer must be caught through logical deduction, not accident, coincidence, luck, or unmotivated confession.

> The killer must be someone who played a prominent role in the plot and that person should be introduced early in the narrative.

> The killer's motive for the crime should be personal, and the killer should be a member of the community, not a professional hitman, bandit, or serial killer.

> The novel should not contain information that isn't relevant to the sleuth, the crime, or the crime's solution. And the method of murder should be rational and plausible enough that a reread would reveal the clues and solution in advance.

> The novel should contain a real murder because it is the crime with the most immediacy and working toward its solution is the best use of the reader's time.

This last rule may be the most controversial since there are plenty of books, such as Janet Evanovich's Lizzy & Diesel series, that use near-deaths, kidnappings, pranks, and thefts as the basis for their mysteries. A book may certainly open with such misdeeds, but there should be a death by the middle of the book (at the latest). In a modern cozy, the horrific mark of death upon such a tranquil and idyllic society is what makes the genre compelling; therefore, not only must murder ensue, but it must be interesting and confounding—extra points if the death affects the proper functioning of the entire community. The severity of life-versus-death stakes and the restoration of justice that's demanded by such a heinous dilemma is the crux of this mystery subgenre. Readers come for the immense catharsis that occurs when evil is narrowly thwarted. Plus, the urgency of murder and the fallout justifies the amateur sleuth's desire and need to become involved in a situation that would normally be out of her league.

So if you're squeamish about the murder rule, consider writing in another genre. This is not a slight on anyone's sensibilities, but a real solution. For example, private-eye novels and police procedurals have a structure that allows for a less severe crime because the protagonists' job descriptions demand they get involved regardless of the stakes. Also, other subgenres like the caper or heist story adhere to a looser set of rules that don't require playing fair with the audience so the immediacy of a murder—compared to, say, blackmail, arson, or accidental death—is not necessary.

Most importantly, all of the rules we just outlined ask that you don't waste the audience's time by giving them a novel that's more trickery than mystery or sending them on a scavenger hunt for clues that aren't available to them. Honor these rules and you're well on your way to writing a book readers will love.

COZIES VERSUS THE OTHER
MYSTERY SUBGENRES

Attributed as being coined by Agatha Christie, the term "cozy" doesn't come from the characters' fondness for drinking tea while mulling over the details of the crime. The word is derived from the small cloth covering used to keep tea kettles warm as the brew steeps. So perhaps, the term is a metaphor for how these more delicately handled bloodless crimes shield us from offensiveness as we mull over the intricacies of the murder puzzle. Who is to say? But I do know this: While many writers use the terms "cozy mystery" and "traditional mystery" interchangeably, there is a slight difference between the stories of the Golden Age and today. Modern cozy whodunits place a greater emphasis on setting, occupation, and interpersonal relationships, and this book will help you boldly build those elements and weave them into the narrative.

It is also worth noting that up to this point, I have been referring to cozies as a "genre," but I want to be clear that they are a subgenre of mysteries as are hard-boiled detective stories, police procedurals, thrillers, and capers. Modern cozies are usually between 70,000 and 90,000 words in length, anything longer or shorter and you may have trouble finding a traditional publisher. Of course, if you are self-publishing, you can drop your range to 50,000 to 70,000 words, but be aware that works under 45,000 are considered a short story or a novella.

Even though the average reader may not be able to articulate the numbers, they can feel when they are being shortchanged. Therefore, indie writers must always let the audience know if they are producing shorter texts because the expectation is for a four-act novel with a full and complete story arc at 50,000 words or more. Unlike indie romances, a cliffhanger ending where the mystery is resolved in the next novel or at the end of a series is unacceptable in the mystery genre regardless of your novel's length or how it's published.

> **Hard-Boiled Detective Novels** – The narrative takes place in a world that starts bad, gets worse, and ends rough. The villain works to throw the loner detective off his trail by force rather than through misinformation and false clues. The resolution may only involve partial justice, and the detective must be willing to get dirty and cross moral lines to get even the smallest measure of satisfaction (*The Last Good Kiss* by James Crumley).

> **Police Procedurals** – The plot involves real police work and guidelines. The main law enforcement elements in the story are not corrupt or inept. They are purveyors of justice, working hard even if they don't always get their (wo)man in the manner expected. The main character is not a loner and uses the resources of his squad (*Still Life* by Louise Penny).

> **Thrillers** – These dramatic narratives rely on intrigue, adventure, and suspense to place the protagonist in dangerous situations that evoke his anxiety and fear while prompting similar reactions from the audience. This subgenre also contains darker elements similar to horror and focuses on the dangers of our world through the vulnerability of an average person attempting to solve a complex puzzle or stop a catastrophic threat. Unlike cozies, these stories don't need to play fair with the audience since the perpetrator is typically known from the start, making the protagonist's goal to successfully fend himself against the antagonist's attacks, cap-

ture said perpetrator, and/or stop the next atrocity (*The President is Missing* by Bill Clinton and James Patterson).

> **Capers**[1] – Written from the viewpoint of the criminals with the central action focused on a series of crimes (usually nonviolent)—thefts, swindles, kidnappings, et cetera—that are perpetrated in full view of the audience. These misdeeds often lead up to some "ultimate score" or an event of great moral reckoning with high stakes and impossible odds. The cast involves a group of light-hearted criminals who may fight at first but whose differences eventually lead to them working together in a manner that either benefits the group or thwarts some adversarial element. The formation of this team is typically the inciting incident, and each member brings a special skill and comic idiosyncrasy to the mix. Law enforcement is portrayed as inept or corrupt and thus the tension comes more from *how will they get away with it* and *what if something goes wrong*—such as a betrayal from within the group or from a collective adversary—than apprehension by the police (e.g. *Diamonds Aren't Forever* by Connie Shelton).

[1]Capers are the angelic twin to heists, which skew darker and typically involve violent crimes with hardened criminals motivated by revenge (e.g. *The Hunter* by Richard Stark).

Hey, What About Suspense?

When we talk about writing a cozy mystery, you of course need suspense. Suspense is defined by *Merriam-Webster's* online edition as "mental uncertainty." In the cozy world, that means our stories should have moments of anticipation or anxiety where the reader believes something perilous will occur. Suddenly, the ordinary appears menacing. That phenomenon is the "edge of your seat" feeling or foreboding you get when you sense something disastrous is going to unfold. In cozies, this can be a moment when it is clear that the sleuth has pressed her luck one time too many.

In thrillers, this is very specifically a moment when the audience is privy to a lurking danger the heroine doesn't have a clue about. Think *Die Hard* when John McClain meets Hans Gruber near the roof of the Nakatomi building and gives Gruber a gun without knowing he's the bad guy. We squeal and yell at the screen because we think our hero has just written his own death sentence.

Even if the scenario doesn't transpire exactly how we anticipate (turns out, McClain gives Gruber an unloaded gun), the technique is used to provide a sympathetic connection between the audience and the protagonist—will he or won't he get out of the impending predicament—while reinforcing the readers' desire to see what happens next. The tricky thing is that when we talk about suspense as a genre, or story category, we are speaking about the term more broadly and must consider what that means for the audience's expectations. In that regard, there are vast differences in execution that prevent us from marketing our cozies as "suspense."

First of all, what people actually mean when they use "suspense" as a genre is really "thriller" because the truth is that any story can (and should!) contain suspense or at the very least tension, which is the anticipation of conflict or an emotionally strenuous situation. For example, in sweet romance, suspense is the will they or won't they overcome their differences to find love. In contrast, this notion of a "suspense thriller" is the overt battle of good versus evil, the detailed push and pull between the protagonist and the antagonist.

That is to say, thrillers emphasize that we live in a dangerous world and that anyone can fall prey to the threat of dark things. This may feel like a nebulous explanation, but it is important to note that the genre evokes the feeling of dread whereas cozies seek to do the opposite. Cozy mysteries want to uplift and assure the reader that all will be well in the end and morality will be restored. The stories are wholesome, bright in tone, equitable, comforting, and the approach of the sleuth is reflection over action.

On the other hand, thrillers are gritty, dark in tone, full of pulse-pounding surprises, and the detective prefers taking action over reflection. In a nutshell, the key difference between cozies and thrillers is that antagonist in a cozy is concealed (covert) until the end while the villain in a thriller is an open (overt) threat that the protagonist actively pursues throughout the narrative.

Naturally, there are novels that cross genres, and I believe my Victoria Justice series is a prime example because it borrows elements from legal thrillers[1] thanks to the law and courtroom procedures I use to fuel the struggle between good and evil. Yet, at the end of the day, my tales are cozy because they adhere to the ideas listed on the chart that follows.

Genre Expectations	Cozies	Crime	Thriller
Murder or Crime	bloodshed takes place off the page or before the story begins	Bloodshed happens on the page	Bloodshed happens on the page in detail
Story Puzzle	whodunit	whydunit	howdunit
Audience Viewpoint	audience plays along with detective but is two steps behind the truth	audience watches action unfold but may or may not uncover the full truth	audience knows much of the truth and many of the dangers but characters don't
Setting	Rural	Urban	Urban or International
Audience Sympathy	logos (intellect)	ethos (ethics)	pathos (emotion)

This chart doesn't cover the full reality of each genre, but you can quickly see why it is unfair to use the term "suspense" as a genre category for cozy mysteries. But as stated before, all stories must have elements of suspense in terms of its dictionary definition of "mental uncertainty."

To build suspense or tension in your cozy, add complications such as putting your sleuth in a dangerous situation that is contrary to her skill set. Give your sleuth a ticking clock or deadline by which she needs to solve her town's murder or diffuse a threat. Add unexpected new suspects, who engage readers emotions with their highly immoral life perspective or mistreatment of the heroine. Consider subverting common plot reveals by hinting that the obsequious brownie baking neighbor may be the killer's accomplice. And definitely, crank up the sensory detail so that every floor board creak or peek around the corner evokes a feeling of danger.

[1] True legal thrillers establish the crime in a manner that allows for a detailed portrayal of court procedure and the politics behind how police, the defense, and the prosecution work together in the name of justice. All of these elements are used to create the story question as well as the thrills. While researchers like Lars Ole Sauerberg, author of *The Legal Thriller from Gardner to Grisham: See You in Court!* (2016), notes legal thrillers can be traced back to the mid-1500's and that the modern format for this genre is often informally attributed to the work of Erle Stanley Gardner's introduction of Perry Mason in *The Case of the Velvet Claws* (1933). Other oft quoted titles for study include *Anatomy of a Murder* (1958) by Robert Traver and *Presumed Innocent* (1987) by Scott Turow.

Recap: Cozies v. Suspense

Although every mystery should have elements of suspense, we should not label cozies as "suspense fiction." This is a distinction normally reserved for thrillers. Cozies focus on the following:

> Crime puzzle
> Motivated amateur sleuth
> Hidden killer
> Cover-up
> Limited suspect pool
> Play fair clues audience must decipher
> Unmasking of the killer
> Restoration of justice

Meanwhile, suspense fiction and thrillers focus on this:

> Test of will
> Hounded protagonist
> Known killer

> Wide scope for good v. evil
> Information given to audience
> Capturing killer or thwarting disaster
> Plot twist and lesson learned

To build suspense or tension in a cozy mystery:

> Add complications to put the sleuth in danger

> Establish a ticking clock to trigger reader dread

> Introduce cagey suspects to keep the audience guessing

> Subvert plot reveals to induce reader shock

> Boost sensory detail to build anticipation

> End chapters with a cliffhanger (just be sure to follow through on the reveal in the next section)

WHAT'S YOUR PREMISE?

Cozies are not stories like *Silence of the Lambs* or *Gone Girl* where the audience spends time in the mind of the killer (or worse, we're misdirected altogether) while the protagonist scrambles for clues. Neither are they stories like Michael Connelly's Harry Bosch books or Louise Penny's Chief Inspector Gamache novels where a professional detective or a series of patrol officers uses standard police procedures to solve a crime.

The central appeal for the cozy mystery, whether written in first or third person, stems from its tight focus on an amateur sleuth whose profession or personality act as the hook on which the mystery typically hinges. So aspiring cozy authors should note, it's not enough to dream up a captivating puzzle or a shocking murder plot, you must also have a high-concept draw that speaks to the audience on an emotional level and you must do so in such a way that the audience can play along with the puzzle your story creates. This is known as your premise.

The premise is the foundation for all your ideas, and the beacon that will guide you as you work. If you can pinpoint your premise prior to outlining or writing, the narrative will be easier to draft because the goals and conflicts used to drive your characters will already be there for you to build upon.

Many cozy mystery advice books will refer to premise as the sub-category your novel will occupy—i.e. *Will my book be a knitting mystery or a culinary mystery?* Naturally, that decision will need to be made, but those considerations don't encompass the full scope of the word "premise." Deciding between a knitting mystery and a culinary mystery is more a discussion about the milieu or backdrop of the story. A strong premise should go deeper—covering the theme, the main character, her goals, her motivations, and the plot's main obstacle. When an author takes the right approach to premise, the result acts as a hook for the reader and a creative roadmap for the writer. And once you start to think of premise in this manner, you'll be able to use my four-step technique to develop one regardless of your story's genre.

Theme and Tone

But first, since the theme is arguably the most important aspect of devising a premise, let's take a few moments to define the term before we delve into the technique of putting everything together.

Theme is defined as the story's main idea or the statement a piece makes about a given topic. An effective theme in fiction also points to what the main character and the reader will learn about themselves over the course of the story.

Even though commercial genre fiction (mystery, sci fi, romance, horror, et cetera) is mainly meant to entertain, it should still center around a theme, philosophy, or morale concept that will challenge the main character and provide an answer to the story's overall question. This can be as basic as "crime doesn't pay," "what goes around comes around," or "love conquers all," but bestselling authors go deeper than this. Be mindful that a story can most certainly have more than one theme and that themes should be universal, meaning they apply to everyone regardless of a person's status or station in life.

Themes are important for cozies because readers often look to the genre to teach them something—if not about a new world or profession than at least about how to better approach life's moral morass—through the social dilemmas experienced by each book's characters. When looking to devise a theme, consider what feelings you have about the topics your story will cover. This is considered the tone you will take toward the work and is conveyed through your diction (word choice) and style (manner of expression).

For example, what are your views on gentrification? How are those views reflected in the story? Does the narrative paint a picture of displacement and disenfranchisement, or does it develop images of progress and upward mobility? Regardless of the tack taken, what do those opinions collectively say?

Once you've recognized what tone the work has taken, be conscious that the theme does not need not be overt and isn't necessarily something the characters are consciously sharing through dialogue and action as much as it is the author's careful use of characterization and setting to convey an overall subtextual message to the audience. Consider the theme something that the author helps initiate but that the reader will ultimately find between the lines as characters encounter obstacles along their tumultuous journey to the conclusion.

You can determine the theme before you begin or craft it afterward with the intention of adding symbols and imagery that align with your overall feelings toward the work. Simply make sure to weave these ideas into the action as seamlessly as possible. You can also use your story's theme to heighten tension by dropping thematic imagery throughout. Thematic tension also exists within the philosophy or outlook of your character via the narrative voice used or their thoughts.

How to Write a Premise

Step 1: Consider your theme. What social problems or issues will your novel explore? How is your story familiar yet intriguingly different than others in the genre? What point will your story ultimately make? What emotional experience will it deliver? And how do all of those answers play into the theme? Brainstorm and write the answers to these questions until you feel you have some ideas that will have the reader leaning forward to learn more. Only then, should you undertake the endeavor of crafting your premise. Establishing that theme early will add context to the dilemma your character must overcome or will be forced to face.

Step 2: Brainstorm your character's internal/external goals and motivations in relation to the novel's theme. Outline these desires and drives using strong verbs. Also, develop a brief description of your protagonist using visceral adjectives.

Step 3: Summarize the specific crisis, obstacle, or conflict your protagonist will tackle during the tale. To do this, imagine a scenario involving your sleuth, then consider what would happen if things went horribly awry. Use vivid detail.

Step 4: Draft your premise using two sentences. One starting with "imagine" and the other starting with "what if." You can eventually put them together as one compound sentence that will become the premise that guides you through the writing process.

Here's an example based on *The Plot is Murder* by V.M. Burns:

> **Theme:** Everyone deserves a fresh start.

> *Imagine* a determined widow finally opens the bookstore of her dreams.

> *What if* the night before her bookstore's grand opening the building's realtor, a man she's known for despising, winds up dead on the back doorstep of her shop?

> **Premise:** Samantha Washington, a widow determined to start a new life, finally opens the bookstore of her dreams, but the night before her bookstore's grand opening the building's realtor winds up dead on the doorstep of her shop.

Here's an example based on my own *Poetic Justice*:

> **Theme:** Speak out for what is right.

> *Imagine* a high-profile judge is murdered during a trial recess.

> *What if* the mousy court reporter, not the attorneys or the police, endeavors to solve the crime?

> **Premise:** Victoria Justice, a mousy court reporter, discovers her mentor—the town's only African American judge—murdered in the courthouse bathroom and must use her trial transcripts to unravel the truth before the killer strikes again.

Here's an example from the film *Minority Report*, starring Tom Cruise:

> **Theme:** The future isn't set.

> *Imagine* a world where crimes can be predicted before they happen.

> *What if* the strait-laced cop in charge of predicting those crimes is accused of murder and has to go on the run?

> **Premise:** Chief John Anderton is the face of the Pre-Crime Program, where violent acts can be predicted before the happen, but when the tables are turned and he's accused of a future murder, he's forced to go on the run to clear his name.

Here is an example from *Dead Until Dark* by Charlaine Harris:

> **Theme:** Discrimination, or don't judge a book by its cover.

> *Imagine* a world where vampires lived out in the open thanks to a synthetic blood supplement.

> *What if* a hunky vampire walked into a bar with a mind-reading waitress?

> **Premise:** In a world where vampires live out in the open thanks to a synthetic blood supplement, a spunky telepath falls in love with a seemingly soulful vampire who brings nothing but death and destruction into her otherwise tranquil existence.

A strong premise should spark a myriad of ideas that you can write down as potential parts of your story. But once you have all of that information, what do you do next? Isn't there a structure we need to follow? Absolutely. That's known as the four-act structure. In the chapters on plot, I will give you that outline as well as the major beats needed to write a kick-butt cozy.

But first, a brief word on hooks.

What's the Difference Between a Premise and Hook?

While some authors may use the terms "hook," "logline," and "premise" interchangeably, I prefer to use the term "hook" in connection with the first paragraph of a novel. Those opening lines should be designed to grab the reader's attention and induce further reading. You know your opening paragraph is strong when it combines plot (physical) and story (emotional) to accomplish the following:

> Raise a story question
> Introduce the protagonist
> Establish a sympathetic connection between the protagonist and audience
> Thrust the reader into the action

To write a good hook, start your story as close to a moment of great change or the inciting incident as possible. Anything too early and you risk boring the audience; anything too late and they might start from a place of confusion. And remember, keep backstory to a minimum. Only add what's absolutely necessary.

With your opening paragraph or hook, you are echoing the premise and making a huge promise to the reader about what's to come. Make sure that you meet those expectations by establishing the tone of your mystery and sticking with the genre conventions until the end. Also, set up your viewpoint. For mysteries, it is best to use only one, either first-person or third-person limited—but again, establish those parameters from word one and stick with it. And of course, make whoever that narrator happens to be as reliable as possible. While there are plenty of fabulous stories that incorporate an unreliable narrator, this is not an element used in the modern cozy mystery.

Here are some questions to consider if you are still having a tough time making that opening paragraph pop.

> What must the opening paragraph or scene provide to give the audience a clear idea of what the book will be about?

> What unusual event, pending problem, or inciting incident should be foreshadowed to draw the reader's interest and keep them turning pages?

> How do I hint at the protagonist's potential investment in this pending event? What are the stakes?

> Is the protagonist introduced? If so, how? And what one or two compelling things do we learn about her?

> What should this opening scene do to establish some early character development for the other main characters?

> Does the work clearly establish the point of view that will be used throughout the first chapter?

> What should the opening paragraph provide about setting—era, customs, season, time of day, et cetera—and how do those elements play a role in the narrative? Have I used all five senses to describe the environment?

> How will the opening line establish genre, mood, tone?

CHARACTERIZATION

In order for the reader to care about your plot, he must care about the people in it. So once you've established a premise, develop your primary characters. Start with the fab four categories that occupy every mystery—sleuth, victim, suspects, and villain. The best way to do this is to complete a character sketch where you outline everything about a character from eye color to their worst nightmare. You can find a sample questionnaire at the end of the section on secondary characters. However, the most important elements of character development are determining each player's overall goal, motivation, and conflict for the story.

In the case of your mystery's protagonist, the goal is going to be some variation of figuring out whodunnit, whydunit, and whether that person will strike again. You will also need to develop a reason, or motivation, for your sleuth's obsession with the case. Consider why solving the murder is important to her. The crime can't simply be another humdrum part of her daily life. It must be personal and it must have long-standing consequences. Lastly, outline what events or forces are stopping her from solving the murder.

Speaking of crime, your next step is to identify the victim. Even if this character dies on the first page of the story, the reader should continue to learn about him throughout the novel by the way the remaining characters talk about him. So be sure to decide how his death effects the community at large. What may help here is to also start brainstorming your suspects to figure out what person(s) could have committed the murder and why.

This bring us to our villain, who should be an admirable adversary for your protagonist—i.e. someone whose skills and/or tenacity could potentially thwart your heroine. The best antagonists are those with a full backstory and a strong motivation for having perpetrated the crime in question. They also need to have a defined place within the community, and it wouldn't hurt if they were somewhat likeable or at least the kind of bittersweet person we love to hate. Think Dolores Umbridge from *Harry Potter and the Order of the Phoenix*.

In addition, you will need to decide why this person has chosen to kill. This motivation can fall within the traditional realms of money, love, power, or fear but should be as detailed as possible. Therefore, you'll need to consider how the villain justifies the crime in his mind. Is he protecting a loved one or righting what he perceives as a societal snub? What event or act turned the villain bad—a childhood trauma or unrequited love? A memorable villain will ensure strong reader investment because the audience will have something substantial to root against.

Now that we've established an overview, let's take an individual look at the characters in your mystery. We will begin with the sleuth—your most important character who must remain active throughout the story—and discuss why it is imperative that this character has flaws. Then we will cover the importance of choosing the right victim and how that leads to the selection of suspects. Next, we will outline the elements needed to craft a convincing killer. And lastly, we will discuss the role of the secondary and minor characters who will flesh out the rest of your story. In a cozy, these people play a slightly bigger role than the average novel since they are part of the beautiful backdrop you want to build to entice readers to return your books again and again.

SLEUTH

"The best crime novels are not about how a detective works on a case; they are about how a case works on a detective."
~Michael Connelly,
author of the Harry Bosch and Mickey Haller series

What Connelly means by this statement is that your detective must be emotionally engaged in the crime they are solving. They should have personal stakes in the unfolding of the mystery. Therefore, it is important that we do more than focus on the plot, or the physical action of the narrative. We should also work hard to ensure the manuscript has a strong story, which is the emotional aspect of fiction.

For example, having the protagonist's boyfriend attacked by an unseen culprit is plot. Having the protagonist wrench at her shirt and scream bloody revenge is an element of story. That is why it is important that your main characters are compelling. Their emotional reactions and personality are what keep the audience invested in your book. In other words, we should feel sympathy as well as empathy for your sleuth.

Before we get into the key elements of crafting the perfect sleuth both physically and emotionally, let's recap some of the characterization basics for the genre. In a modern cozy, the protagonist is typically a female amateur sleuth age 30 or older to align with the middle-aged women who are the most avid readers of the genre. She should be unique and engaging, usually through the creativity of her profession, and should be relatable in her characterization—think archetypes such as the girl next door, the survivor, or the lovable screwup. Although she may appear to be an ordinary person, she should have extraordinary sensibilities or skills that fuel her desire for detection and make her the perfect person to take over the crime from the police. She also needs a strong moral compass, a willingness to analyze things that others ignore, and the mental fortitude to see the situation through to the end. She should have a strong reason for getting involved in the crime—be it personal or professional. But most importantly, she should have a personal wound that she will overcome during the course of the narrative, ideally one that prevents her from seeing the solution to the story question until she's able to conquer the wound.

Now, let's build on that foundation of cozy characterizations. Your protagonist should be driven by her inner conflict, which often takes its cue from the theme (or vice versa). For example, if your theme is *what goes around comes around*, your protagonist may grapple with a past misstep that's come back to haunt her. Basically, your sleuth's inner conflict speaks to the character wound she will need to overcome by the end of the story. If you do your character work properly, your villain or antagonist will also have his own inner conflict that leads to a character wound; however, he won't be able to overcome this block by the end of the story thus leading to his downfall.

Here are some questions that will help you get to the heart of your sleuth's characterization:

> Who is your sleuth?

> What is her occupation? Why does she work in this particular vocation? Brainstorm a profession outside of law enforcement that will intrigue the reader, encourage world building, and introduce multiple characters as potential suspects.

> How does she become involved in the murder investigation?

> What is at stake if the sleuth fails? Livelihood? Limb? Life?

> What are her goals for this book, and what are her long-term goals for the overall series arc?

> What is her personal wound?

> What skills does she bring to the investigation, and how do they relate to her profession and personal wound?

Remember, when thinking about your sleuth in terms of the crime, treat the murder with the danger and high stakes it deserves to help pump up the tension and suspense of the story. Also, give your main character a strong internal conflict, wound, phobia, or dark past because it becomes the emotional element that fuels her proclivity for detection while also challenging her ability to solve the crime. This emotional flaw or physical imperfection will give dimension to the plot and allow for character growth over the course of the story as she slowly learns to face her fears and conquer the wound that's been holding her back.

Next, make sure she has a job or social circle that brings her in contact with a large portion of the community or give her a believable inside connection that allows her to traverse between her world and the world of the crime—a lover, best friend, or nemesis can act as a bridge in that regard.

Even though we want our heroine to succeed in the end, she should falter throughout and eventually succumb to the worst-case scenario. After all, no one is invincible. Besides, invincibility is boring. Even Superman has weaknesses, and the best stories allude to those weaknesses even when the hero wins. This can come in the form of the heroine's self-doubt or taunts from her peers (and the villain) that reveal the hero's physical limitations. This balancing act keeps the audience engaged and brings much-needed tension to a subgenre that is otherwise known for its tranquility.

Sleuth in Action

An amateur sleuth narrative has four elements it must establish before fully immersing the main character into the mystery. First, the sleuth's crime solving abilities must be identified and her background outlined so that any relevant skills are discovered and highlighted before they are needed. The audience should ideally see the sleuth's intelligence and charm work under normal circumstances before applying them to the problems brought on by the local murder.

Second, when the crime occurs, the sleuth should initially refuse to get involved. This could be as simple as the matter being too dangerous and thus better suited for the police or the sleuth having another agenda they deem more important, that is, until something changes to draw the protagonist into the investigation.

Third, a strong motivation to take the case must be cultivated—whether the sleuth herself is accused of the crime and must clear her name or the murder befalls a loved one.

Lastly, the sleuth needs a significant reason why she's refusing to let the police handle the investigation on their own. Perhaps, the cops are looking at the wrong suspect or consider the case a suicide. Either way, your main character should have some piece of concrete evidence at the start of the investigation that proves the police have it wrong and can't be trusted to catch the killer.

Side note: Law enforcement in cozies is usually portrayed as corrupt, inept, or ineffective thereby forcing the sleuth to rise like a superhero to take the charge since there is no one else capable and willing to handle the responsibility. Therefore, after crafting your sleuth, you will need to take a moment to identify the sources of power in the world the sleuth occupies and devise different ways for her to obtain the knowledge and resources normally reserved for those within that system. Does she have a special relationship with the police department secretary and as result gets the latest intel on the murder? Did she go to high school with the police chief and so uses his most embarrassing moment to extort a case detail or two? You get the picture. But again, before your sleuth takes an active role in the mystery, she should first have a significant clue and theory that law enforcement can't or won't investigate further.

Recap: Sleuth

In addition, to whatever process you're using to brainstorm your basic character sketch. Answer these questions about the sleuth to jumpstart your cozy.

Name:

Age:

Profession/Ambition:

> What unique setting does this job suggest?

Appearance/Talents:

> What eccentric bedfellows or coworkers or admirers do the afore-mentioned occupation attract to the sleuth?

Personality/Preferences:

> What intriguing homestead, community, town, or dwelling best suits (or ruffles) the main character's sensibilities?

Personal Wound or Blindspot:

> How could this problem both help and hinder the protagonist in solving the murder?

> Why is the sleuth interested or invested in solving this mystery?

> In what way are the police acting inadequately so that the sleuth is compelled to get involved?

> What's odd about the murder to the sleuth? Why isn't it an open and shut case—or if it is, why does the sleuth disagree?

VICTIM

You may recall from the recap at the end of the chapter titled "Mystery History," that one of the common conventions of the modern cozy is to have a despicable or unlikable person act as the victim. As noted in that section, the advantage in having a despised victim is that this ensures everyone will have a motive for wanting him dead. The disadvantage is that you've relegated the character to being a mere plot point who lacks dimension and fails to garner sympathy. Some writers consider this disadvantage a minor setback since an unsympathetic victim ultimately keeps the reader focused on the puzzle and prevents the lighthearted cozy from getting too emotionally dark.

However, I'd argue that since the goal is to make our stories as rich and complex as possible, your modern cozy does not need to be as tightly bound to the idea of an objectionable victim as the stories of yesteryear. The choice is up to you. At the end of the day, what we really want are strong characterizations for all involved. Experiment with what complements your book's premise and seize any opportunities that will make the audience work a little harder to ferret out each of your mystery's twists and turns. But keep in mind, whether they're naughty or nice, the personality of the victim should contribute to their demise along with their occupation, social ties, personal history, or anything other reasons you can squeeze in there. Bottomline, this death shouldn't be random.

Consider these questions when creating your victim:

> **Who is the victim in the community?**

> Why is the victim killed? What motive could each character have for wishing the victim dead?

> What happened leading up to the murder? How is the victim killed?

The first three questions set the framework for the sleuth's investigation. The last two flesh out the novel's background and help develop the early expository scenes crucial to the opening setup of your book. So let's go through each question.

Who is the victim in the community?

In terms of prewriting, this is about finding ways give the victim a strong connection to the sleuth so that the protagonist has a convincing reason to move forward with solving the crime. You also want to give this person enough clout or connection to the overall community that each suspect will have some sort of relationship with them whether it be familial, business, or personal. What role does this person play in the community? How does their death affect the sleuth and the town at large?

Authors have two approaches to fleshing out the victim. We can either spend a decent amount of time getting to know the victim, which delays their death until the end of the first act. Or we can delve right into the murder from the very first chapter allowing the other characters to flesh out the victim's history. We'll call these approaches "viewed victim" and "non-viewed victim," respectively.

Viewed Victim

In some mysteries, we see the victim prior to his death, and that behavior may provide clues to the murderer before the sleuth officially starts her investigation. This is a great way to insert some of your larger clues without giving away the ending, and I encourage you to see the chapter on clue placement for more details.

Having the victim alive for a few chapters, also allows for the element of surprise regarding who gets the axe and garners audience interest and sympathy for the deceased character. That is to say, if we give readers a little time with the victim to learn about their behaviors and passions, then the audience will be doubly invested in finding the killer when that person dies. The audience will also better understand why the sleuth would want to get involved and be more sympathetic if the character is one that's meant to be liked or revered. Showing the victim's relationships with other community members in real time will give you freedom from bulky backstory during the detection portion of the narrative because the suspects won't need to recall every detail regarding the nature of their relationship with the deceased. We'll have seen some of it, so the story doesn't get bogged down and can keep its momentum as the plot thickens.

Non-Viewed Victim

Other stories open with the murder and thus mainly present the victim as a corpse. Any characterization provided comes in the form of statements and recollections by the other characters. This can lead to factual intel, but could also result in unreliable, misleading, or contradictory information. Fortunately, these skewed perspectives prove helpful in hiding clues, setting up plot twists, or inserting the occasional red herring. Just keep in mind that having little to no page time with the victim limits the scope of real-time storytelling for this character and sets them up as a mere plot point. This often places the manuscript in a position of telling rather than showing when it comes to key events like what happened in the hours leading up to the murder. Therefore, when using this approach, work doubly hard to keep the story active and the pace constantly moving forward.

Why is the victim killed? What motive could each character have for wishing the victim dead?

Regardless of whether you show your victim alive ahead of time or not, the narrative will be enriched if the reader can relate to the victim, so create some sympathy for that character. Otherwise, if readers don't care whether the victim is dead, they might not care about the crime's resolution. And if a mystery reader doesn't care about the crime, you've already lost them. The best way to remedy this is to create a compelling background for your victim, either by keeping them alive long enough to be thoroughly introduced—perhaps giving the sleuth a problem or malady that the victim's eventual murder further complicates—or by making them a significant enough pillar in the community that everyone has an opinion about them. Just avoid flashbacks. Cozy mysteries do best when they convey present-day action or work with witness accounts that ultimately act as clues.

What happened leading up to the murder? How is the victim killed?

Here's where we must maximize our creativity because the victim and his method of death can be just as much of a reader draw as the sleuth. Since cozies don't depict the violence on the page, you're free to pick any mode of death you'd like. You can fuel this brainstorming process by considering the setting and the social and economic background of the community. What prevailing civic philosophy helped open the door for someone's potential to kill? As long as the murder is plausible and well-motivated, you're welcome to go over-the-top. Consumed a casserole of catnip and broken glass? Drove the family sedan into the community pool? Hung from a hot air balloon? The sky's the limit! No pun intended.

But with that said, here's an essential note: Avoid anything that's offensive, reminiscent of torture, or associated with a serial killer such as mutilation, rape, cannibalism, pedophilia, et cetera.

Also, even though you're not showing the gore and violence, the discovery of the body will still be an essential scene you'll need to plan in advance. That is to say, you don't want to get too graphic, but you also don't want to completely relegate the crime to an exposition-filled offstage moment such as, "Did you hear what happened to the Sheriff?" The discovery of the body and the initial (false) assumptions about the murder are a key element of the plot because they act as the inciting incident for the protagonist turned sleuth. Therefore, work to place such scenes fairly early in the story—shoot for around fifty pages or three chapters deep.

Recap: Victim

Name:

  Age:

  Occupation:

  Appearance/Personality:

  Role in the Community:

  Relationship to the Sleuth:

> How and where does this person die?

> What act, profession, relationship, habit, or personality trait put this person on the killer's radar?

> What secrets did this person keep?

> In addition to the character's background and the means and mode of death, consider how the victim's body will be discovered and who makes the discovery.

KILLER

Character work for the killer should be as extensive as the work done for the sleuth since the murderer's actions help drive the story and his motives contribute to the shocking conclusion. Even though the killer's identity is concealed until the end, this character should be in plain view from the very beginning yet be someone the audience would never suspect. Deceit should be the murderer's modus operandi.

Thus, the murderer is only caught because of his ego, arrogance, paranoia, or a personal flaw he cannot see past. Whichever aspect you choose, that element should fester within the killer as the sleuth draws closer to the truth. Another reason for capture may be that the bad guy kills again or attacks the sleuth in a hastily devised plan to misdirect the investigation, yet the act eventually has the opposite effect and leaves behind clues that clarify his involvement in the initial murder. Basically, the killer's capture should never be a matter of coincidence or stupidity on his part. Both the killer and the sleuth must try their hardest to evade and capture, respectively, until the very end.

Of course, elements of the crime should hint at the killer's identity. For example, who among the suspects is strong and agile enough to kill a college wrestler with their bare hands? The sleuth should also seek to reason through similar concepts when reviewing the time and place of the crime along with the weapon used thus setting up the parameters for means, motive, and opportunity when interrogating witness and checking alibis.

But let's get back to characterization, answer these questions when crafting your killer:

> **Why did the murderer choose to kill?** Avoid generalized motives like keeping the town's peace. This should be a personal reason like the killer having his business ruined by his wife's ex-husband.

> **How did the murderer choose to kill?** What method was used?

> **Why does the murderer choose to kill now?** Was the incident planned or a crime of passion? What about the events of the current story forced him to act today instead of years prior?

> **How do the murder's deeds initially elude the police?** Remember, in order for the sleuth to get involved, she must see something the cops are missing. So what is it about this crime that has everyone fooled except your sleuth?

In addition to thinking about these questions when brainstorming your character sketch, you must also ensure that the answers appear on the page. This information should be revealed in clue form over the course of the book or unfold in a revelation upon the unmasking of the killer or be explained during the denouement and resolution chapters of the novel.

Even though you won't show the actual murder in your story, you must have a clear idea of what happened on that day and the steps the killer took to cover things up in the moments that followed. To do this, decide what clues or elements of the crime the criminal could have left at the scene and what he could have accidentally (or intentionally) taken with him. For example, the murderer could unknowingly <u>leave</u> wool fibers from his sweater, dirt from his shoes, fingerprints, or the scent of his cigar. He could also unknowingly <u>take away</u> pet hair, dry wall dust from a room under construction, or blood on the cuff of his shirt.

Another element you'll need to tackle when creating your killer is to make sure he has the motive, means, and opportunity to commit the crime as well as an alibi that initially makes him look innocent. Even if you're a pantser, deciding this information prior to writing is essential because all decisions thereafter will stem from this baseline.

> **Motive** is the actionable idea or reason to commit the crime.

> **Means** is the ability and resources to commit the crime such as access to the weapon or knowledge about the mode of death.

> **Opportunity** is the time to commit the crime unseen, i.e. an unencumbered chance to follow through on intention.

> **Alibi** is the proof of having been elsewhere during the commission of a crime or any circumstance that seemingly prevents someone from having committed a murder.

Clearly defining each of these for the killer will give you a solid structure for the murder and a roadmap for building clues as the plot moves to its conclusion. You can also plot in advance how this person will get caught, i.e. how his alibi will be upended, since this will also help with clue placement during your outline.

For the sake of clarity, let's elaborate on our discussion of motive, means, and opportunity in terms of how these concepts play into misdirection and obscuring the identity of your killer.

Motive and Means

"Motives for murder are sometimes very trivial, Madame."

"What are the most usual motives, Monsieur Poirot?"

"Most frequent—money. That is to say, gain in its various ramifications. Then there is revenge—and love, and fear, and pure hate, and beneficence—"

~Hercule Poirot in Agatha Christie's *Death on the Nile*

Murder motives, while abhorrent to those within the story, usually speak to a universal idea that the reader can understand and somewhat empathize with the killer since we've all had painful or disturbing conundrums that have pushed us to the brink. That's why the motives most often used can be broken down as clearly as they have been by master detective Monsieur Poirot. Once again, those reasons broadly amount to money, love, power, and fear. We can break them down further into things like hate, envy, rage, protection (self-defense or otherwise), concealment (for other misdeeds), greed, revenge, and shame. However, all of those things fall under the big four.

While it is okay to plot your story so that any of your suspects could have committed the crime, you must have a definitive killer in mind for the end reveal and you must provide a specific reason the murder happened during your telling of the tale rather than before or after the plot depicted in your novel. And of course, that killer must have a strong personal reason for having taken the life of another person. A private hardship such as having their business ruined drives the killer into the desperate deed. Cozies don't have random crimes, homicidal maniacs, or sociopathic serial killers. Rather, the murder is a selfish act meant to fulfill a specific need that outweighs the pain of hurting others and the agony of getting caught.

Whatever the motive may be, make it logical, discoverable, and relevant to the current events unfolding in the present reality of your story. Decade long grudges or obscure links to characters who never appear on the page lack the urgency necessary to keep the reader invested.

Lastly, be mindful that the means, or the ability to commit the crime, makes sense for the person chosen as your killer. For example, don't make the method of murder be that the killer dragged a hundred-pound anvil up a flight of stairs and dropped it on the victim's head on-ly to find that the culprit is an 80-year-old woman. That set up is pos-sible, but not plausible. Readers will scratch their heads and be unsatis-fied with that reveal. You must set up the means and resources for the crime so that it makes sense for the character. So if you have a mode of death that requires strength or specialized knowledge, such as the mix-ing of deadly chemicals, be sure to put that skill or ability in the history of one or two of your characters so that the method of murder makes sense once the killer is revealed.

Opportunity and Alibis

Opportunity is not just access to the victim but also access to the weapon, scene, and enough time to commit the crime. Think of op-portunity as the period of time when the killer has a chance to follow through on his intentions.

If a person can prove they didn't have the opportunity because they were nowhere near the crime scene, it means they have an alibi and are often removed from the suspect list even if they have the other two ele-ments of motive and means. Alibis are often the component the sleuth must discover or disprove to separate the guilty from the innocent. Be advised that establishing an alibi for any of your characters first starts with outlining the indisputable elements of the crime like the time of death or the location of the murder.

Second Murder

The second murder is usually a coverup by the killer to sow chaos, scare the detective, cast blame, or shut up a key witness. This is often a crime done in haste with little to no coverup. But if premeditated, the crime could very well take the form of a deceitful murder where an attempt is made to make the death look like the product of something else like an accident or suicide.

Misdirection: Obscuring Your Killer

Here are some examples of the different ways you can obscure the identity of the killer by diminishing his role as a suspect. In these scenarios, the killer deflects his involvement by pinning his deceitful actions on someone else or by asserting the truth of his actions in a manner that makes their actual execution seem silly or improbable. I encourage you to go wild with your imagination on this front. Examples are included for clarification, so please accept my apologies in advance for spoiling the endings of some popular books and films.

> The most obvious person did it, but evidence is planted in such a manner that this suspect initially seems too overt to the point of unbelievability or appears to have been framed (e.g. *A Murder is Announced* by Agatha Christie).

> The murderer convinces everyone he was the real murder target, usually with a faux attack on his life, thus shifting blame away from himself, removing his name from the suspect list, and casting doubt on another (e.g. *Ten* by Gretchen McNeil).

> The person assisting the detective is actually the murderer (e.g. *The Murder of Roger Ackroyd* by Agatha Christie).

> The murderer is the initial suspect, but he is cleared early in the story only to be found guilty for certain at the end (e.g. Wes Craven's *Scream*).

> The killer is actually a murderous duo who work together to provide alibis for each other (e.g. *Death on the Nile* by Agatha Christie).

> An authority among the characters declares a certain person could not have done it for either a logistical or physical reason and thus shifts blame away from the actual culprit (e.g. *A is for Alibi* by Sue Grafton).

> The killer is the victim who works with an accomplice to plan his own murder (e.g. *One of Us is Lying* by Karen M. McManus).

A final point to note about writing a killer in a cozy is that unlike thrillers or mysteries with a harder edge, both the killer and the victim need to not only have standing in the community and a connection to each other, but their presence and eventual absence must have an emotional or psychological impact on the sleuth and the overall story. That is to say, characterization, civic connection, and the story's environment are essential. Create a world that is large enough that each character's on and offstage life—work, school, marriage, et cetera—could play a role in the victim's downfall and the killer's motive.

Recap: Killer

Name:
   Age:
   Occupation:
   Appearance/Personality:
   Role in the Community:
   Relationship to the Sleuth:
   Relationship to the Victim:

> What is the killer's goal? What is the killer's motive?

> Why is the killer killing? What drives this person to kill (money, love, power, fear)? Is there a life event or particular incident that leads the killer to violence?

> How does the killer justify the crime in his or her own mind or attempt to justify it to others?

> Create a timeline of actions for the killer even when he is not on the page to ensure that his means and opportunity align with what's presented by the sleuth in the finale.

SUSPECTS

Look to build a closed circle of suspects. This can involve centering the story on a club, workplace, or familial gathering. As noted earlier, a great example is the White House Chef Mystery series by Julie Hyzy. Even though the books take place in a large city, the stories focus on a specific group within a larger work environment. Each character who ends up on your sleuth's suspect list should play an active role in the community and have some sort of connection or history with the other suspects and victim so the protagonist can follow leads that may help her smoke out the killer.

Structurally, suspects should provide the detective with clues or information either through an interview or their behavior. The extracted content should propel the investigation forward, or act as a misdirect (deliberate or unintentional), based on each character's level of withholding information or perpetuating lies. Initially, each suspect will want to partially coverup their connection to the deceased even if innocent. Suspects may do this to prevent revealing an embarrassing secret, to protect a loved one, to hide their own attempts to solve the crime, to avert retribution from the murderer, or any other number of personal reasons.

Therefore, it is important that your suspects are fully developed characters and not mere ciphers the sleuth sifts through to find a solution. They should have goals and motivations just like the other main characters in the book. Consider what each suspect wants out of life and give them a secret related to that concept which they are trying to protect. This will provide each suspect a clear motivation for how they interact with the sleuth. For example, a suspect harboring news of an affair may be hostile while a suspect who disliked the victim but stands to gain coveted real estate may be overly cooperative. Use your suspects' goals and motivations to help build conflict between them and the sleuth.

	Suspect 1	Suspect 2	Suspect 3
Motive			
Goals			
Secrets or reasons they may be dishonest to police or sleuth			
Reaction to accusation or questioning			
Strategy for keeping their secrets or defending their honor			

If this chart isn't inspiring enough on its own, picture your collection of potential suspects and ask each of them the following set of questions:

> Who is this suspect to the victim, the community, and the sleuth?

> Why does this suspect want to see the victim dead?

> What does this suspect stand to gain or lose from the victim's death?

> Where was the suspect during the murder? What's their alibi? Do they have the means and opportunity to commit the crime?

Secret and Lies

To add layers of tension and suspense to your mystery, each suspect must have at least one secret that makes them look guilty whether they are actually involved in the crime or not. These secrets should help move the mystery forward by sending the sleuth in a new direction for her investigation with each new reveal. Most secrets may be red herrings but at least one should hint at the killer's identity.

> **An example of a secret that acts a red herring:** A man lies about his whereabouts on the night of the murder because he is having an affair.

> **An example of a secret that points to the crime's culprit:** A man lies about his whereabouts on the night of the murder because he is being blackmailed by the killer to provide an alibi for them both.

The point of a good secret is to make the innocent look guilty during the main detection section of the novel. This can be as obvious as having one of your suspects threaten the victim in a public forum minutes before his death (then have him refuse to say why) or identifying what appears to be a duplicitous motive for one of your suspects (e.g. a CFO stands to take over the business from his deceased partner). However, if you prefer something more subtle, review some of these other ways to shine the lamp of suspicion on innocent characters. Be advised, you don't have to use them all, one or two will do.

> **Uncooperative Behavior:** Create a suspect who flees when approached for questioning or pleads the fifth when it comes to her involvement. Or better yet, a suspect whose statements don't jibe with her behavior like a woman who claims to be a vegan but is seen eating a McRib.

> **Unusual Evidence:** Create a suspect who is observed purchasing, using, or carrying the murder weapon or other elements thought to have been used to conduct the crime.

> **Unruly Bedfellows:** Create a suspect who is himself a known liar and criminal or who hangs out with unseemly characters and is hence assumed guilty by his association with bad people or bad vices such as drugs. Similarly, a person previously questioned or convicted for a comparable crime would make an equally shady character.

> **Unlikely A-holes:** Create a suspect who is seemingly sweet then makes an unlikely turn like punching a nun or having a history of sex addiction. The juxtaposition of this double-sided coin not only lends itself to potential guilt but also keeps everyone guessing.

You will, of course, as the story concludes need to have a valid explanation as to how or why each suspect engaged in such questionable conduct.

Number of Suspects

How many suspects should a writer include in their mystery? As a general rule, cozies work well when there are at least three and no more than five. Any less and the murderer becomes obvious. Add more and you run the risk of confusing the audience. But the reality is that the setting of the book may dictate the size of the suspect list just as genre affects word count.

For example, if you are writing a howdunit like a locked door mystery, you could have just one suspect since those narratives typically begin with a strong suspicion toward a specific culprit. The police are stumped as to how the killer executed the crime under impossible circumstances, causing your sleuth to step in and discover the methods used by the allegedly guilty individual. On the other hand, if the story is set on a cruise ship where the sleuth is on vacation, the number of suspects could rise upward of eight people.

Consider this list to determine the number that suits your needs. Just remember the suspects should be varied enough to keep the audience guessing until the end.

> Traditional mystery (Golden Age): 5-8
> Modern Cozy (whodunit): 3-5
> Mystery with thriller tendencies (whydunit): as few as 3
> Impossible Crimes (howdunit): as few as 1

Regardless of your selection, create a diverse range of suspects from those who obviously wanted the victim dead to someone who unwittingly stumbled upon the crime scene. And no matter who these people are or what they do for a living, make sure they each have a secret, crime related or otherwise. Secrets give each character motive to lie to the sleuth and adds a layer of fun story problems that require solving prior to the murder. The suspects should also all know each other so that correlations can be made and blame can be laid.

Recap: Suspects

Start with the chart provided earlier in the chapter to create your suspect list then fill out a character sheet for each person. Use the categories below to make your suspects as well rounded as possible.

Name:

Age:

Occupation:

Relationship to the victim:

Relationship to the Sleuth:

Role in the Community:

Motive:

Opportunity:

Lie told about their role in the crime:

Secret that makes person seem guilty of the crime:

Secret that makes person seem innocent of the crime:

SECONDARY CHARACTERS

After completing the character sketches for your fab four, you'll need to create secondary characters, i.e. the folks who will surround your sleuth and aid in her detection efforts. Start by brainstorming the people who would realistically be in her life—mother, lover, best friend, et cetera. Then think about the additional skills your sleuth will need to solve the mystery and assign them to the people on the aforementioned list. Even if the characters themselves are not aware of how they enhance the sleuth's abilities, you as a writer should cast your story with people who provide your sleuth will additional knowledge and access. This may mean giving your sleuth a best friend who is a doctor so that your sleuth can better decipher the autopsy report that her boyfriend, who is a janitor in the coroner's office, steals to get a better understanding of the victim's murder. See where we're going with this?

Again, just be sure to make these people fully developed characters with their own goals and motivations. Even better if you can make some of those goals conflict with what the sleuth hopes to accomplish to provide challenges and develop subplots.

Remember, personal relationships and emotion play a much bigger role in the modern cozy than the traditional stories of the Golden Age when mysteries by their very nature were a reflection of social formality and class hierarchy—maids, butlers, heiresses, country estates, wills, et cetera. So be sure all of your primary and secondary characters have an internal and external conflict as well as a personal connection to the victim, suspects, killer, and type of crime.

In fact, the personal/professional life of the sleuth and the social or communal setting are often the main draw for contemporary readers, so make those elements shine and give every character a reason to exist that goes beyond being a source of information. Have them provide comic relief or tension or give them interesting personality quirks. Allow them to act as a sounding board or a sage, particularly those secondary characters who will follow your sleuth from book to book if your concept develops into a series.

Here is a list of the archetypes mystery writers commonly use to occupy their novels. These are simply the basis for characters who are used throughout fiction because of their universal appeal. Naturally, you will need to build on them and add your own spin.

Sidekick: This can be a loyal confidant who acts as a supportive sounding board—like Lula does for Stephanie Plum in Janet Evanovich's iconic series—or this person can be a foil whose lifestyle and choices are the mirror opposite of the protagonist, offering a sneak peek of what might happen if the sleuth takes the wrong path.

Mentor: Consider this a motherly or fatherly figure who imparts wisdom or a word of warning to the main character. They don't have to be older just wiser in the ways of the world and can be anyone from a boss to a neighbor to an actual teacher.

Love Interest: A character of this nature is self-explanatory. And since love is a universal concept everyone can understand and rally behind, adding this emotional element makes for a great subplot and has the potential to add stakes if this loved one comes under fire from the villain.

Fool: A more apt description for this character is one who provides comic relief, but it is also someone whose less direct and more humorous delivery enables the sleuth to hear some of those hard truths she may not want to acknowledge but desperately needs to survive.

Nemesis: For the sake of emotionally compelling fiction, the main character should have someone in her life who challenges her or forces her to work harder like a braggadocios coworker or elitist neighbor. This person may look like the killer or villain on the surface. In reality, he or she is essentially good person who drives the protagonist mad due to their opposing viewpoint. To be clear, the nemesis and the antagonist are not the same person. In fact, if your mystery is a series, the nemesis is a person who can continue to appear from book to book while an antagonist is one and done. The role of a good nemesis is simply to make the main character work harder and to help her see things in a new light by providing additional internal conflict and external frustration.

Since cozy mysteries usually revolve around the sleuth's profession as a baker, knitter, interior designer, et cetera, readers expect to experience the larger community in which the sleuth lives. So show your main character's family, coworkers, sorority sisters, and local politicians to create depth to the world you're building and provide additional resources to your character. Use this as an opportunity to further develop your sleuth's milieu—whether those people show the softer side of your sleuth's otherwise gruff exterior, help provide access to the police's investigative materials, or act as soothsayers among uncooperative suspects who peddle in secrets and lies.

Recap: Secondary Characters

Up to this point, I have given you questions to consider that speak directly to the roles of sleuth, victim, killer, and suspects. But if you don't have a general character questionnaire, use the one below to make all of your characters as well rounded as possible.

Full name
Age
DOB
Birth place

Eye color

Hair color and length
Height
Weight and build
Favorite or key gestures
Other distinguishing marks

Occupation
Education
Marital status
Children
Favorite color, food, hobby, music, movie

Life goals (deepest desires):
Biggest fear

What happened in the past that hurt them or made them who they are today?
Favorite childhood memory
Worst childhood memory
What does the word "mother" mean to you?
What does the word "father" mean to you?
Worst habit
Past relationships

Religious values

    Core values (What drives this character? Why? How?)

    Biggest secret

    Biggest regret (If you could change a past decision, what would it be & why?)

    Greatest strength

    Greatest weakness

    Secrets or secret shame

What do they need, even if they don't realize it yet?

    What do they believe to be true about themselves because of a past pain?

    What are they most afraid of due to that pain? Worst fears?

    How do they portray themselves to others? What armor do they wear to protect themselves?

    What is their true self? Who are they deep down?

THE CRIME

Murder creates a highly emotional conflict that cannot be undone or atoned for by simply attempting to mend or return what is lost. The punishment for such crimes is severe, so the killer has ample reason to be at his most duplicitous in evading capture.

> **Overt murder** – no attempt made to make the crime look like anything other than a crime

> **Covert murder** – an attempt is made by the murderer to cover up the death

> **Deceitful murder** – an attempt is made by the murderer to make the death look like the product of something else like accident, self-defense, act of God, suicide, et cetera

Recognizing which category your crime falls into will help shape the look and feel of the people on your suspect list in terms of their means, motive, and opportunity for murder. This may also affect back-story, particularly for the victim and killer as the two should have an intertwined personal history. Work to deliver the unexpected. When we develop the circumstances surrounding a crime, the reader will build assumptions about what happened, much of which—if we do our jobs as authors right—will turn out to be false.

Once you have devised the main elements of the mystery—crime, killer, victim, sleuth—tie them together so that the story built on this framework makes sense. Remember, the murderer in a cozy works to create a false reality, so think about your crime in terms of what the killer has done to **cover up** his tracks. Consider how the sleuth may interpret those clues to come to her initial **theory**, and determine how the coverup and theory diverge from the **truth**, which has to be revealed in full by the end of the story.

We must structure our stories so that all three things are happening simultaneously. Even if the audience isn't consciously aware of all three aspects, we must plot our stories so that we know the timeline behind each layer.

> **The coverup** - what appears to have happened
> **The theory** - what the sleuth thinks happened
> **The truth** - what really happened

For example, all of the time and place elements in your story are aligned so that the killer really could have snuck into the kitchen unseen and added poison to the cocoa because everyone else was distracted trying to catch the pair of wild turkeys that someone (again, the killer) let into the house. Basically, the main storylines that we experience throughout the book (the killer's cover-up and the theory) should ultimately complement the truthful solution in a manner that leaves the audience saying, "Aha! I didn't notice that in the moment, but that explanation makes sense in retrospect."

POINT OF VIEW

Another way cozies seek to expand upon traditional mysteries and the fair play rules is point of view, or the perspective from which the story is told. Think of this as the story's narration. Viewpoint plays a crucial role in determining the overall effectiveness of character development by providing the perspective through which the audience observes and experiences the events of the narrative.

Because modern cozies generally use the sleuth's first-person or limited third-person viewpoint, today's audiences never need to decipher what the investigator is thinking through the filter of a secondary character or omniscient narrator. These close viewpoints aid in cultivating reader intimacy. However, this was not always the genre's standard.

Detective fiction as we know it began with Edgar Allan Poe's short story, "The Murders in the Rue Morgue," published in *Graham's Magazine* in 1841. Poe's story invents the basic plot repeated throughout detective fiction—the sleuth's associate narrates their collective adventure, and the pair use research, interviews, and reasoning rather than brute force or physical violence to solve the crime. This reliance on intellectual tools resonates throughout the work but is somewhat diluted by the use of a narrator who is not the sleuth, which distances the audience from the detective's true process.

A similar narrative technique is used in Anna Katharine Green's *The Leavenworth Case* (1878), which is considered the first full-length American novel to bring this form of detective mystery to the forefront. Green's story is set in New York City and revolves around the murder of a prosperous merchant in the library of his mansion. The book introduces Detective Ebenezer Gryce although the tale unfolds from the viewpoint of Raymond, a lawyer who represents the deceased. Since the lawyer in *The Leavenworth Case* is a family outsider looking in, we can only see a small portion of the crime from his skewed perspective.

With each new clue, his knowledge grows, but we do not get the full picture from the mouth of the expert investigator until the end. For the most part, this technique of having a supporting character lead and shape the narrative through his first-person viewpoint succeeds, but the technique presents a major problem if the audience gets ahead of him. A sidekick narrator who is slow or bumbling may cause the audience to lose interest. The author also runs the risk of creating a point-of-view character who becomes a mere conduit for exposition or a narrator whose sole purpose is to ask naive questions of the superior sleuth. Both of these outcomes are tedious and make the audience aware of the filter through which the story unfolds.

To avoid this problem, the modern cozy has shifted the narrative voice to the amateur sleuth whose proximity to the crime and vulnerability about its difficulty is much more accessible to the audience. This also establishes that the novel will be a character-driven tale and gives the reader an intimate perspective into the sleuth's psychological journey. Although this may initially feel limiting to you as a writer—since with first-person and third-person limited the sleuth can only describe events she experiences firsthand—this inability to see from multiple angles will aid in maintaining the book's tension (the protagonist won't know what's coming next, so neither will the audience) and make it perfectly clear which parts of the puzzle the audience should take seriously.

While some may see this shift to a more humanizing viewpoint as a dilution of the genre, modern cozies use these changes to build a more complex narrative and subvert the idea that the common (wo)man must wait for some mastermind detective to take control. The amateur sleuth can be her own hero—and by extension, the reader can be his own hero. This allows cozies to reinforce the mindset that the average person has the ability to rise to the challenge of extraordinary circumstances—a valuable lesson in our self-made society and one that keeps bringing readers back to the page.

Types of Viewpoints

In fiction, who the author chooses to tell the story can have just as much effect on the plot as the action that unfolds. That is to say, our stories are always relayed to us by a narrator. That speaker's voice establishes the novel's tone, i.e. the story's outlook or attitude toward its subject, as well as provides a distinct opinion of the events and other characters that inhabit the fictional landscape. This perspective, also known as point of view, works like a personal camcorder, recording the action and defining the framework through which the reader will view things. What this narrator chooses to focus on through her viewpoint, and where she is positioned in the story, will ultimately shape what we know, what we feel, and what we care about as the novel develops.

Consider these three commonly used types of narration. Each of these viewpoints will help you determine who is telling the tale, who the story is about, and the level of information your audience will have available to them. Decide which narrative approach is best for the story you'd like to tell and pick one for the backbone of your novel. New mystery writers should stick to one narrator and one narration type throughout even though it is possible to use multiple viewpoints and narrators that change from scene to scene or chapter to chapter. However, since your main focus for a cozy is playing fair with the reader, use the viewpoint that will best allow the audience to follow along with the clues.

Of course, if you are advanced and choose to use multiple viewpoints or several narrators, be sure to have a significant emotional or character-driven reason for doing so. Also, make sure you've mastered your knowledge of the different types of narration so that you're not popping in and out of various viewpoints mid-scene—that's a huge faux pas in that will make your writing appear amateurish, so avoid it.

Third-Person (he, she, they)

There are three main types of third-person narration—omniscient, objective, and limited. Each supply the reader with various levels of information. An omniscient narrator has access to the thoughts and actions of several characters at any place and time. In fact, she can view the same character both internally as himself and external through the eyes and emotions of another character in a later scene because this narrator is all-seeing and all-knowing. While this is helpful in painting a picture, it makes it tough to hide things in a whodunit without feeling like you're playing a shell game with the audience. Where's the mystery in that?

One positive aspect of the omniscient third-person viewpoint is that it allows the narrator to interpret and comment on characters' behaviors for the audience thereby giving the reader insight into what things could mean for the protagonist and the story as a whole. However, comments and opinions from the narrator tend to be intrusive and distance the audience from the story. The reader may feel as if they are watching actions unfold rather than being a part of them.

In contrast, an objective narrator views characters' behavior from the outside and has minimal insight into the various characters' thoughts and feelings. This means the text can only imply what characters might be thinking or feeling through their speech and action. Unfortunately, this lack of emotional output may prove detrimental to fostering audience empathy in a genre fraught with peril. So let us consider our final entry, the limited third-person narration, which is the third-person form most often used in mysteries.

The scope of third-person limited includes the thoughts, feelings, and behaviors of a single person. The narration provides the reader full access to one set perspective—ideally that of your sleuth. The audience can move through the fictional world with the POV character experiencing only those sensations in her vicinity without knowing what those around her are thinking—just like real life—but still allows the author an opportunity to write from a broader perspective since the story is being narrated rather than dictated by the main character. This point of view also has the added benefit of creating a bit of distance between the reader and the audience compared to first person. But for that reason, this viewpoint might make establishing reader empathy for your sleuth more difficult.

First-Person (I, me, my)

This is an intimate perspective that facilitates the reader's understanding of the point-of-view character by having the audience take residence inside the narrator's head. We see a single person's thoughts and actions as if we are that person. Thus, character intimacy is immediate and the author has an opportunity to create a unique voice for the protagonist since there is no filter between the sleuth and the audience.

But the advantage and disadvantage to this is that the narrator can only report what she perceives with her five senses. Thus, the audience's view of each scene remains limited to the sleuth's viewpoint as she strains to see in dark alleys or finds herself locked out of a room where a crucial battle is taking place.

Sometimes this limited perspective can lend to the tension in a mystery, but this inability to see the full picture can also create plot problems if your story has multiple characters in numerous locations engaging in varied activities all at once. To put it plainly, if the first-person narrator is not there to see something, it's like the event never happened for the reader or must be later relayed to the POV character by another player. This recollection of facts has the tendency to slow the pace and turns part of the novel into a story within a story. Combat this problem by keeping your sleuth at the heart of the action.

Despite this potential drawback, many mystery writers use first person because it allows the audience to build an immediate bond with the narrator and creates the illusion that the pair are working together to solve the crime. Be mindful this puts the onus on the author to create a main character likeable and interesting enough that the audience is content to stick with them for the entire story. One way to do this is to make sure something funny, tragic, or thrilling is revealed about that person in the hook.

Another first-person pitfall is that the viewpoint tricks some writers into using thought more than dialogue. Fight this tendency by making the sleuth active in her investigation with constant questions for those in her sphere of influence. If an inner monologue is necessary, make the event active by having the protagonist debate an issue with herself or work to cope with an internal conflict caused by another character's transgressions.

Unreliable Narrator

Lastly, first person is the viewpoint of the unreliable narrator. While this isn't something a writer should concern herself with when writing a cozy, it is a concept worth learning about since the reality is that a single character's subjective perception prevents the reader from ever having a completely accurate picture of events. In other words, no one ever sees things as they genuinely occur.

However, as long as you play fair with the reader, this shouldn't be of great concern unless you actively plan to implement an unreliable narrator, which is used to great effect in other genres. For example, books like Gillian Flynn's *Gone Girl* take this literary device in a deliberately duplicitous direction where the two narrators deceive for self-preservation and a malicious intent. Other narrators may gain the distinction of unreliability by having naively or unintentionally provided some falsehood or misconception to the audience based on the way they view the world—e.g. *Perks of Being a Wallflower* by Stephen Chbosky (suppressed memory), *The Curious Incident of the Dog in the Night-Time* by Mark Haddon (the naivete of youth + Asperger's syndrome), or *The Girl on the Train* by Paula Hawkins (impaired alcoholic memory).

But for novels in general, and with cozies in particular, the expectation is that the first-person POV character is giving an honest account of events. As the author, you may further verify this by having the other characters in your story corroborate your protagonist's version of reality.

Recap: Point of View

Point of view will shape every facet of how you tell your story. So to find the proper viewpoint character, ask yourself: Whose journey will the novel most closely follow? Then consider whether first- or third-person best suits the story you're trying to tell and that character's role in the narrative. Most modern cozies tell the tale from the perspective of the sleuth, which should make choosing the viewpoint a cinch.

Regardless of the viewpoint used, only one technique and one person's viewpoint are necessary per scene. As a beginner, avoid the temptation to mix first- and third-person in the same novel. Sure, this tactic can be done successfully as with *V is for Vengeance* by Sue Grafton. But if you're not a bestselling author, you run the risk of alienating your audience who then has to decipher structure rather than falling in the love with your cast. Instead, focus on your protagonist, eliminate any viewpoints that diminish that focus, and master the basics of one POV before bending or breaking the rules.

A great book to read if you'd like more information on this topic is *The Power of Point of View* by Alicia Rasley.

Tense

Along with viewpoint, verb tense has an impact on the story. Because most fiction narratives are a recollection of a profound event, authors typically use past tense (-ed) for their work. This is not to say that present tense isn't acceptable as it does lend the sense of urgency one would expect during the life-and-death situations common in a cozy. However, past tense remains the tradition almost as if to provide a subconscious indication to the reader that everything will work out in the end.

SETTING

Setting is the unifying element of a story. By tying time, locale, and culture into a one milieu, setting can convey a mood, mirror a theme, or provide an obstacle for a character's behavior. A vivid setting is an integral tool in capturing an audience for a cozy mystery. The setting should almost become a character who the audience can turn to for comfort. They should be convinced that this tale couldn't take place anywhere else, and they should be seduced to return to the locale (and hence the series) again and again.

Your setting should also enrich the novel's tone, characterizations, and plot. Build these setting details by weaving them into the scene through the viewpoint character's mood and actions. Your sleuth's reasons for undertaking the mystery should also help reveal elements of the setting and vice versa, so think of character building and world building as a symbiotic relationship.

To put it another way, a novel begins with the character's ordinary world, and the conflict that emerges widens that person's worldview so that the setting expands as well. With a stellar setting should come growth, and it is up to you to create a setting that is dynamic enough to undertake that expansion. Think carefully about how the era, season, and geographic location will affect your characters' mindsets, values, and work ethic.

In my contemporary courtroom cozy series, the Victoria Justice Mysteries, the titular character is born and raised in a small seaside town set near the Atlantic Ocean and Delaware Bay even though she is described as having aquaphobia. Thus, the tension that comes with having to conduct an investigation through her fear forces her to face her demons and become stronger by the story's end.

So can you see how a mystery setting should significantly shape your characters' decision making and personal lives throughout the tale? Don't choose a setting at random or make broad choices without considering the overall impact on each character's development. Ask yourself: How does your sleuth's perception change because of the setting?

Modern cozies often incorporate the protagonist's career and personal life as the backdrop for the tale. This is an opportunity to introduce the audience to the activities and traditions commonly found in that field. For instance, my series is about a court stenographer who investigates murders, so a large part of the series takes place in the courthouse and includes trial etiquette and procedures.

As you create the outline for your story, make a list of locations and backdrops that will enhance the storyline. For instance, a modern-day shrimp boat captain turned amateur sleuth in Sarasota, Florida, would have scenes at the fish market, along the docks, and mid-deck of the trawler in the Gulf of Mexico. Mystery readers love a location that has a cultural or regional flare, so use setting to provide nuance that teaches the audience something new about the geography the characters occupy.

Setting Considerations

Here are some key elements of setting to consider during the initial stages of your prewriting.

When will the narrative take place?

> Consider the time period (contemporary or historical) and time of year (season).

> What do characters do for fun? (e.g. ski v. surf)

> What do characters complain about? (e.g. women's suffrage v. marriage equality)

> How do characters dress? (e.g. bustle dresses v. hoop skirts)

> How do characters detect? (e.g. deductive reasoning v. forensics)

Where will the narrative take place?

> Consider the geographic location (country, province, state, city).
> How do characters speak? (accent v. dialect)
> What do characters consume? (pop v. soda)
> How do characters travel? (the subway v. the tube)
> How do characters interact? (NYC brusque v. southern hospitality)

What makes the setting unique? Why does the story unfold here rather than elsewhere?

> What is your sleuth's occupation and the backdrop or culture for that profession?

> Is there hierarchy?

> Are there special procedures?

> Does your sleuth's trade have jargon or equipment that will need to be explained to the audience?

> Do the characters have a dress code? Is there a social or cultural meaning behind this style of dress?

> Does this profession or locale have unique rooms or build-
ings that will act as a backdrop?

Be specific about the choices made in each of these categories as
they should both narrow your story's focus to a specific era and aes-
thetic while at the same time enriching those choices. Basically, your
answers should significantly influence the novel's plot. For example, a
story set in modern-day Harlem during the Christmas holiday with a
Black female jazz singer as the lead will unfold differently than the same
premise told in 1920s Harlem.

Also, be mindful that even what feels like the smallest shift in setting can have vast consequences. A story set in Hollywood, California,
during the Golden Age of Cinema in the summer of 1955 has a vastly different history to pull from than one set in Oakland, California,
during the same period since parts of that city had begun to engage in
the early Civil Rights Movement. Even stories designed to reflect our
modern landscape can vary if we're not specific about the date. For instance, life pre-smartphone in 1998 is vastly different than life post-
smartphone in 2008.

However, this is not to say that every aspect of your when, where,
and what has to be based in reality. You can always place a fictional
town next to an actual one or add a made-up trend or technology to a
very real cultural phenomenon as long as your new details align with
what the audience already knows. In either case, do the proper research.

What actually may prove most difficult in the setting department
and most telling for your characters are the personal spaces associated
with each player such as their homes or offices. Think about what those
spaces should express. If your main character is in mourning due to
the murder of a spouse, maybe his or her bedroom has grown cluttered
while preoccupied with the loss. Also, consider the details of their profession—is this person's job entry level with a cramped cubicle, or is it
an executive position that includes a corner office? Large or small, every

choice made for the setting should mirror the character's values and station in life.

Be as specific as possible with your setting, but at the beginning of your series, be careful only to describe the part of a town, building, or office that serves your current narrative. Taking this approach, leaves the door open to add additional locations to your city's map as the characters' talents and storylines develop. You don't want to be in a situation where the second book in your series requires a hotel on the town square, but your first book describes that location as containing nothing but law firms.

And if you choose to use real locations, research those settings online or create a hands-on experience for yourself so that you can describe these locales and customs with some sense of expertise. Just don't use your research as an excuse to avoid finishing your masterpiece.

Mood

Mood is a narrative's atmosphere and is often created by both the setting and the attitude the point-of-view character takes as she describes the locale. Other elements that help establish mood include weather, time of day, music, and sounds. We see mood played to great effect in film with noirs being dark and sultry while romantic comedies are colorful and upbeat. We can still do the same with our fiction by getting specific about the methods we use to describe each character's surroundings.

A Word About Description

Description should serve the action unfolding in a story. Great writers ensure their description serves more than one purpose. Remember, you are not just setting the scene or conveying pretty images, you are moving the plot forward by placing the reader in the story, developing character, creating tension, establishing a problem, providing motivation, outlining a goal, et cetera. Use the entire SEED to grow your description.

> **S is for Sensory:** This type of description to relies on sensations or information collected through the five senses—sight, sound, taste, smell, and touch.

> **E is for Emotional:** This type of description uses personal feelings, reactions, passions, and responses to outside stimuli and internal recollections.

> **E is for Expressive:** Use this type of description to show imaginative or emotional awareness expressed by figurative language or creative wordplay.

> **D is for Data:** Use this type of description to convey statistics, facts, rigid details, or scientific evidence to enhance the reliability of your point of view.

Remember, the protagonist's point of view aids description too. Instead of just setting the scene by reporting the facts, let the character's thoughts filter through the description to show more about the hero based on his interpretation of the world. Include memories and associations borne of his experiences and expectations. This boosts the effectiveness of the description and aids characterization.

Analyze the descriptive elements of the authors you love. Discover how they use metaphor, action, and sensory data to describe their settings and characters in a manner that evokes feeling and propels the scene. Have behavior be the bedrock of your descriptive elements and avoid descriptions that read like an inventory or laundry list. Have a reason or purpose for every description and ensure those descriptions feed characterization and the action. Then continue using those elements of description for each character or setting throughout the story.

The Power of Images

Imagery in the literal sense is a descriptive marker for anything that can be seen or felt with the senses—auditory, tactile, visual, gustatory, and olfactory. Yet, stylized descriptions can be used to evoke emotional and symbolic meaning for the reader. Images involve emotion without telling. They can enrich subtext, plant clues, foreshadow, and add misdirection that leaves the reader guessing and eager to find out what's next. A good image resonates and evokes a feeling in the reader. Imagery can also draw a reader's attention to theme or demonstrate a character's true nature. In that way, imagery is synonymous with symbol since imagery can foreshadow events and direct a reader's focus to a specific aspect of the tale.

Recap: Setting

S.S. Van Dine states in his essay "Twenty Rules for Writing Detective Stories": "A detective novel should contain no long descriptive passages...no atmospheric occupations." This is another mystery convention that has changed over the years because the modern cozy is expected to have an enticing audience setting, preferably one with scenic views. In fact, setting has become one of the genre's main draws with audiences often falling in love with the cultures created by these uniquely warm but universally familiar locales. Of course, these settings should have a small town feel or communal aspect where the pool of suspects remain small. This closed community could be a drama club on a college campus or a church in a mid-western suburb. Let your imagination run wild.

But regardless of how you choose to tackle setting, the world should still be large enough for new people to pass through or for you as the author to alter the backdrop to better fit the crime and align fresh suspects as needed. For example, consider how the Southern Vampire Mysteries by Charlaine Harris jump from Bon Temps to Shreveport to

Dallas as needed to add new characters to the plot but always remains aligned with the tight communities of Sookie's friends and the secretive world of vampires, shifters, and weres.

As you begin to work on your setting, think about the following: What makes your setting unique? This is especially important if you're using a city or state often fictionalized—locales like Florida, California, New York, and Massachusetts. How will your setting elements play a role in the story? What world does your sleuth inhabit? Is it an industry-based world like catering or interior design? Or a hobby-based world such as quilting and scrapbooking? Maybe your cozy takes a historical slant and depicts America in the 1920s during the Harlem Renaissance? Whatever you choose is up to you. Just be sure you let the setting influence your sleuth as much as your sleuth influences the setting.

CLUES: THE KEYS TO UNLOCKING THE MYSTERY

"Clues are the traces of guilt which the murderer leaves behind him."
~Marie F. Rodell, *Mystery Fiction: Theory & Technique* (1943)

What is a Clue?

Clues are *evidence* that provide insight which leads to the solution of the crime. Work to create clues that unveil something specific about the who, how, and why of the murder. They can be objects, an action, speech pattern, or scientific fact, but they must be concrete. Here are a few quantifiable elements that work well as clues for detection:

> Location and condition of the body
> Objects found at the scene of the crime
> Time of death
> Distances
> Fingerprints, footprints, tire treads
> DNA – hair, fibers, dead skin, follicles, bodily fluids
> Alibis
> Records, reports, finances, letters, new clippings
> Texts, tweets, social media, computer data
> Eyewitness accounts, phone calls, recordings

Feel free to use your imagination here, but be forewarned...

What is NOT a Clue

Hunches and instincts are different from clues. Clues must be specific and concrete. To create great clues, consider things that are measurable or provable against a pre-defined norm. Also, shy away from merely relying on the killer's potential means, motive, or opportunity as your only clues. Those elements aren't genuine clues as much as they are the sleuth's main guideposts for weeding out suspects. Stick to the list above when establishing the clues you'll use to shape the story and guide the reader.

Below, you will find a list of items that don't meet the criteria for clues. Of course, you may include some of these elements to make your story more interesting, but your sleuth shouldn't rely solely on intuition for the entire novel.

> Speculation
> Lies
> Guesses
> Gut Feelings
> Confessions
> Dreams

Where to Find Clues

Clues can be found almost anywhere. A clock broken in a scuffle can speak to the time of the murder. The before and after conditions of a sealed room can speak to the crime being an inside job. Eyewitness accounts can provide clues as to the habits or physical traits of the suspect. Explorations of the crime scene can produce insight about the condition of the body, the murder method, and modes of attack. The possibilities are endless. Be creative. Just remember that every killer, by the very nature of occupying the space where the crime is committed, takes something away from the scene as well as leaves something behind.

Once the investigation has begun, have each scene contain a clue or red herring. You can make each clue as obscured or obvious to the audience as you choose, but the sleuth should be actively working toward gathering these pieces of evidence as they move toward the crime's solution. Also, the answer to the story's puzzle shouldn't be so obvious that readers can determine the outcome without the main character's investigation and interpretation of the clues.

To embed a clue into a scene, consider who the sleuth would need to interview or be interviewed by to drop the hint or relevant information needed to move your story forward. Weigh this against what the sleuth would need to know going into the scene, and decide how this fresh news will affect the sleuth going out of the scene. In other words, what will be the result of the scene, and what will the sleuth then need to know or believe to reach the next destination in her search for answers? Of course, the scene will need to have a conflict too. Never lose sight of goal, motivation, conflict (GMC). The idea is to insert clues into the protagonist's quest to achieve the story goal, which should be some variation on learning whodunit.

How to Use Clues

The dissemination of clues will help to hide and eventually reveal the killer's identity. The best clues are often hidden in plain sight either because that essential information is provided before it's needed or it's shoved in the middle of a long list of nonsensical things, but the easiest way to organize the distribution of clues is to think of them as three main types—real clues, revealing clues, and red herrings.

Real clues speak to the killer's motive and help the sleuth solve the puzzle. Revealing clues are those that provide a turning point in the plot like a second dead body or a confession that doesn't quite add up. Red herrings throw both the audience and the detective off the trail.

Use all three clue types liberally throughout to keep the audience guessing and to help with pacing since every mystery runs the risk of devolving into a boring series of question-and-answer sessions.

As you're writing, set your real clues throughout the manuscript using the art of clue placement. During the detection portion of the manuscript, the larger more revealing clues will come into play. And of course, when the killer is trying to deceive the sleuth or you as the author want to slow the audience's discovery of information until the final act, set up clues to misdirect or act as decoys.

> Clue placement (hiding real clues)
> Clue used for detection (revealing clues)
> Clues used as deception (red herrings)

Look at these each category closely because how you use each concept will determine whether the audience gasps with delight saying, "Wow, what a clever ending. I didn't expect that killer, but it makes sense considering the clues," or hisses in disdain griping, "I saw that ending coming a mile away."

Clue Placement (Hiding Real Clues)

"If a clue leads directly and unequivocally to the suspect, there is no room left for mystification." ~ Marie F. Rodell,
Mystery Fiction: Theory & Technique (1943)

The key to clue placement lies in putting the clues in plain sight but in a manner that allows them to go unnoticed by the reader. This doesn't mean alter the truth or exaggerate portions of the intended idea. This is a matter of misdirection in the same manner used by magicians. Select what elements to show and which to conceal, then consider how those choices impact the scene's purpose and pace.

Below, I have listed several ways to insert clues into your dialogue, action, and overall storyline without making them obvious to the reader while still playing fair. These techniques will give your mystery a more organic feel and make the puzzle aspect of your narrative more fun.

> Expose one or two clues before the crime is committed so that the audience isn't 100 percent aware of their importance.

> Squeeze clues into petty arguments or place them in a line stated by minor characters.

> Introduce a factual statement during a funny moment. The humor will undo the gravitas of the clue, leaving room for the reader to overlook the importance.

> Place key information in the mouth of a child or a usually unreliable witness so that the audience overlooks the possibility at first glance. A great example of this can be found in *Crooked House* by Agatha Christie.

> Show the sleuth accusing the wrong character of the right crime or the right character of the wrong crime.

> Present clues out of order so that their collective meaning is more difficult to decipher.

> Deliver the clues through a character who is a braggart, gossip, or blabber mouth so that the clues become part of the constant chatter that person provides whenever they are on the page. Their words become so trivial that both the reader and the sleuth fail to pay full attention.

> Reveal a big flashy clue then place several smaller more powerful ones thereafter. The ah-ha moment of the big clue

will overshadow the smaller ones or fool the reader into thinking they are less important.

> Break a big clue into several small parts and scatter those chunks throughout the story to make it difficult for the reader to grasp the full meaning of the clue. Many authors cut their star clue in half, giving one part of the reveal before the murder and the second half of the reveal after. Similarly, you can note a clue at the start of the novel and not have that idea become relevant until the murder. Any of these approaches can work for an issue you'd like to give a slow reveal.

> Let the absence of clues become a clue. This can include missing items or things the murderer stole from the scene as well as the failed execution of a common routine or pattern. For instance, the fact that the normally rowdy family pet didn't bark when the murderer entered suggests that the killer was someone familiar to the household. "The Adventure of Silver Blaze" by Arthur Conan Doyle contains a scene where Sherlock Holmes famously unveils such a clue.

> Drop the clue in the middle of a list of mundane things so that it goes unnoticed.

> Distract from the clue by having a major action sequence, like a chase, occur to pull focus from clues exposed before or during the pulse-pounding moment.

> Highlight an obvious clue, but endow it with two possible meanings that point in opposite directions. That is to say, interpret the same clue in two different (but plausible) ways so the audience becomes split in their thinking. But be mindful

to clear up this disparity as the story builds to its resolution and the killer is revealed.

> Use the audience's core assumptions and prejudices against them as means for concealment. Consider this riddle: Mr. Smith and his son Arthur were driving in a car. The car crashes. Mr. Smith is killed instantly, and his son is rushed to a local hospital. The old surgeon at the hospital says, "I can't operate on him, he's my son Arthur." Have an answer? If you're stumped, it's probably because you're assuming only men can be old surgeons. Of course, the riddle primes your mind for that type of thinking by highlighting the gender of the first two characters. The answer is actually quite obvious. The surgeon is Arthur's mother, but note how the riddle uses a common misconception to misdirect. You can do the same with your mystery and succeed in hiding pertinent clues in plain sight.

> Have a suspect provide half-truths. However, you must be careful here because the detective cannot be the character who does this, and those missing elements need to eventually come to light through active detection from the sleuth. In other words, a suspect can lie or slightly alter the truth, but the detective cannot because they are the medium through which the audience gets all their information. Any falsehood on the part of the sleuth throws the audience completely off the trail—and remember, **one of the main rules of the cozy subgenre is that we must play fair with the audience** so they can take part in the fun of solving the puzzle.

Clues Used for Detection (Revealing Clues)

In the last section, we outlined ways to hide clues in plain sight. This is important because we want the audience to slowly piece together the truth alongside the sleuth. To play fair, the reader must be privy to all of the same information as the protagonist and learn that information at the same time. Don't have your main character commit the sin of omission where she realizes something but doesn't explain it or uncovers something so obscure that the audience couldn't possibly have common knowledge of it without proper explanation.

Next, decide how the protagonist will go about collecting these clues. Is she stubborn and moving forward bullishly despite warnings from those around her, or is she sneaking around covertly gathering information along the way? Knowing exactly what about the current action resonates with the sleuth's wound or internal conflict will determine what motivates the sleuth to take action and determine her approach for clue collection.

To produce high-quality clues, you'll need to create believable ways for your amateur sleuth to logically gain access to police department records, news outlets, media resources, and medical examiner information. The sleuth may also need to comb through the victim's personal belongings at their home or office. Depending on the crime, the sleuth might also want to view the victim's body and crime scene. This may be tricky if your sleuth wasn't present when the deceased was found. In such an instance, make sure to provide access to the coroner's office or devise a trustworthy witness who can relay a full account of the body's condition and its location.

But regardless of how the sleuth gathers her information, she must point out clues as they appear. To do this, have her engage in the following process:

React to the clue⇨ Analyze the clue⇨ Draw a conclusion⇨ Produce a theory

While the behavior of your characters and the events of your plot will put a fresh spin on this formula, this sequence should happen upon every new discovery. Sometimes this can happen in a few words. *Wow, look at those footprints. They're leading from the window. That must be how the killer got inside.* Other reactions and discoveries may take several pages. Play with the variations as the story permits.

Also, keep in mind the sleuth's analysis, conclusion, and theories don't always need to be 100 percent accurate. Of course, it helps if most of them are, and they should definitely become more accurate as the story progresses and she gains a larger number of reliable clues. See the chapter on detection for more information about analyzing clues and producing theories.

But again, how you execute this process depends on your personal flair. The only non-negotiable aspect to this formula is that the sleuth must **always** have a quantifiable reaction to each **real** clue as a way to signal the audience to take note. This clarion call can be done in dialogue or through the protagonist's internal musings, and can be anywhere on the scale of "Hmm" to "OMG!!!" BUT, it must be done in such a way that the audience is never in doubt about what something means to the sleuth. Remember, this is how we adhere to our fair play rules.

However, you are welcome to vary the level on those reactions to add a slight misdirect, if desired. For example, maybe the sleuth isn't aware how important a missing letter opener is at the time she discovers the fact, so her response is small even though that's ultimately the key to the entire case.

Clues Used as Deception (Red Herrings)

Red herring refers to the smoked fish dragged across the trail to throw dogs off the scent of the animal they are supposed to be chasing. In mysteries, a red herring is meant to have the same effect of misdirecting the reader. This is a clue that provides a temporary distraction from the solution to your mystery. Unlike standard clues, red herrings work hard to get the audience's attention.

These clues can be tangible or intangible (or even a person!), but it is recommended to use red herrings sparingly so as not to discourage the audience and to maintain an overall level of fairness to the story's puzzle. Remember, your goal is to deceive, not confuse.

But what makes a red herring work? Basically, the result or reveal attached to the truth behind the red herring either needs to lead to a dead end or further complicate matters. Here are two ways to set up a red herring:

> Establish a series of obvious clues ousting a suspect as the murderer only to have that person's potential guilt raise a whole new series of questions.

> Reveal a secret that on its surface appears to be the key to the murder when in reality it is a small part of a larger truth.

Here are four ways to resolve a red herring and forge ahead to the truth:

> Provide an emotional appeal from the suspect that demonstrates their inability or lack of desire to hurt the victim.

> Kill the accused suspect. This indicates that they couldn't have been the killer but their mode of death should reveal more about the killer.

> Introduce concrete evidence that points to an alternate theory and clears the suspect.

> Indicate that the clues aligned to accuse a specific suspect or induce a specific theory are all clever maneuverings by the killer.

Tangible, Intangible, and False Clues

Tangible clues—i.e. things you can analyze or experience with the senses such as fibers and fingerprints—often hint at where a suspect may have been. This type of clue is usually something the suspect inadvertently took with him from the crime scene such as blood splatters on a sleeve or something that they unconsciously left behind like pet hair or cigar smoke. These clues can help to tie characters to a specific location, establish a connection between two characters, or narrow a timeframe.

For example, if the murderer left behind muddy footprints, we can conclude the crime took place after midnight because that's when the rainstorm began. Or if the victim's shirt is missing an oddly shaped button and that item is found in a suspect's room, we can assume those characters interacted the day of the murder. Of course, the clues themselves aren't a sure-fire sign of guilt, your sleuth will still need to make deductions and draw correlations for the audience.

Also, be aware that clues go beyond the crime scene. An author can place clues throughout the story—before or after the crime—and within multiple areas of the community based on characters' relationships. In other words, don't feel like you need to limit yourself to elements tied directly to the night of the murder. Subsequent events and attitudes can assist in unraveling the crime, which brings us to our next type of clue: intangible clues. These are things that are legitimate evidence but lack concreteness such as local history, data, or an eyewitness statement.

For instance, learning that a local flower shop recently ordered the exact pesticide poison used in the murder brings up the questions: Who owns the shop? Why the coincidence? Or if a fastidious grandmother's gardening trowel is discovered missing. The question becomes who moved it and when, and does its blade match the victim's fatal wound? Both situations are stellar intangible clues that can lead your sleuth in several directions for her detection. Ideally, such evidence should lead the sleuth from the clue to a potential suspect and then the crime. Whereas, the previously mentioned tangible clues will generally lead the sleuth from the crime to a possible suspect.

Intangible clues: suspect⇨crime
Tangible clues: crime⇨suspect

Characters can also exhibit physical traits, habits, or behaviors that act as clues and speak to possible guilt. These move like intangible clues from suspect to crime and have the advantage of being a subtle but fair way to hide your murderer in full view. For example, if the victim is killed with a pair of left-handed scissors, have one of your suspects engage in behavior that shows him hiding the tendency to favor his left hand. Or on the flip side, if you have a suspect who has the known character trait of fainting at the sight of blood, the sleuth may rule that person out as the killer.

Lastly, false clues are a mix of tangible or intangible elements specifically engineered by the killer to draw attention away from his deceitful behavior. He may disrupt the proper interpretation of a clue (e.g. plant the victim's unique shirt button in his best friend's kitchen) or create a scenario that implies his innocence (e.g. prove he couldn't have stolen grandma's trowel because he was out of town) or conceal the truth of a clue by distorting, damaging, or misplacing the info or item (e.g. burn down the flower shop so its invoices can't be collected by the police).

Think of false clues as one way to introduce a red herring, but be warned: As the person creating the story, we don't ever want to solidify ideas that are wholly untrue. All clues, even the false leads, must have a seed of validity to them. Your job as the author, if you choose to create such a misdirect, is to create a situation or plant them in such a way that the audience doesn't immediately see the relevance or attaches the wrong meaning to the otherwise true information provided. If you find yourself only able to sustain the mystery through a series of wild untruths without the introduction of any new and vital information, rethink your storyline and clues as there may be a larger plot problem.

How Many Clues Do You Need?

Well, that's really up to you. The more clues that are planted the easier it is for your audience to solve the crime alongside your sleuth and the more satisfied they will feel at the end of the novel when all is revealed. As a general rule, you should have at least one clue for every deduction or major discovery the sleuth makes. However, as long as you play fair with the clues provided, you could get away with creating a mystery that has only a handful of clues. Of course, those clues would need to speak directly to unveiling the killer's means, motive, and opportunity—specifically, why he committed the crime, how he did it, and what he did to cover it all up.

Grow Tips: Clues

> Remember, any clue that requires additional knowledge about an obscure or unknown subject (like geocaching) should either come with an explanation or generate a scene where the sleuth looks up the definition so the audience has everything they needed to properly examine the clue.

> Clues are the roadmap to the final conclusion, so make sure you've plotted that journey accurately. Although you may work to initially jumble or obscure those hints, they must come together at the end to reflect the sequence of events on the night of the murder, and the sleuth must share that revelation with the audience.

> Avoid developing scenes whose sole purpose is to introduce a clue. Doing so, is like pointing a flaming red arrow at the element and will overemphasize its importance. Not to mention, it makes for a boring and predictable novel. A well-

written scene should have a compelling conflict that serves multiple plot points and pushes the story forward.

> Weave clues into every possible nook and cranny of your text. It's easier to hide a clue in a cluttered room rather than an empty table. In other words, don't just rely on one element to mask clues. Shove hints into action, behavior, setting, characterization, et cetera.

PLOT STRUCTURE

Cozy mysteries are a form of commercial fiction. This means there are a basic set of reader expectations and plot points that must be met for the story to qualify in this particular category. Here is the basic layout, which you could consider the plot map or beat sheet for a standard cozy. Put your own spin on each element to make them your own.

Be mindful that each act will vary in length. The fourth act will be the shortest while the second act may prove the longest as that's where the sleuth begins her detection. Also, be mindful some of these plot points would need to be expounded upon or eliminated altogether if we changed from a cozy mystery to detective fiction or police procedural or thriller. Therefore, this is by no means meant to be a catchall plotting guide for fiction writers in general.

Act I: Setup

> **Introduce the sleuth, her profession, the setting, and situation**
> **Introduce the victim and the killer**

- Obviously, we won't know who the killer is at this point, but we do need to have whoever the killer is walking among the characters in Act I. Don't wait until the end or middle of the book to introduce that character. As stated during the section on fair play, we must give the reader an opportunity to successfully play along. That means having the correct killer be one of the potential suspects from the start.

> **Introduce who finds the body**

- Many authors tend to make this person the sleuth, but this can be anyone.
- Cozies are also expected to have the death occur in the first act. Ideally, this should occur in the first fifty pages.

> **Reveal the murder scene and provide initial clues that something is "amiss" (establish tension by foreshadowing conflict)**

> **Unleash the disaster or discovery that forces the sleuth to take the case and actively investigate**

- This should always be the element that closes the end of the act.
- Even though the sleuth doesn't commit to getting involved until the end of the first act, the investigation may already be in progress by the police or others and you are welcome to start adding clues from the first page.

You can always revisit these as the story unfolds, but fleshing out these elements is where every mystery starts. The opening scene should give us the main character's name, gender, physical appearance, personality, profession, and relationships with (or opinions about) those in her peer circle. However, don't feel you need to place all these things in a big introductory paragraph like Sue Grafton does her early alphabet novels. Cozies play things subtle. Drop hints lightly throughout like breadcrumbs in the forest so that readers are eased into your new world.

Grow Tip: Act I

Most mysteries have a point in the middle of the first act where the crime has been uncovered yet the sleuth refuses to get involved. This initial refusal often appears to underscore the sacrifice that's involved, the seriousness of the dilemma, and what the sleuth will need to overcome in herself to succeed at the task. It's up to you whether the sleuth fully understands the gravitas of the situation, but the audience should because throughout the first act you've been crafting the plot in a manner that makes the stakes clear.

Having a first refusal is also good practice because it's realistic. A private citizen wouldn't get involved until it is clear that the police are bungling the investigation, so the event that causes the sleuth to take the case should occur at the end of the first act. Common reasons include the sleuth or a close friend losing money, their business, or their freedom. Other more serious ones, especially if your choice is to combine this "decision to get involved turning point" with the "discovery of the murder inciting incident," is that the sleuth or a close friend gets hurt, murdered, or accused of murder.

Act II: Detection

> **Identify suspects and engage in interrogations**

> **Plant clues**

> **Introduce subplots (love, personal growth, ailing parent, et cetera)**

> **Evasion or flight by suspects (or killer may strike back with an attack or second murder)**[1]

- Again, we won't know who the killer is at this point, but they should still be actively covering their tracks and throwing obstacles in the sleuth's way that cause calamity. This is the portion of the story where the sleuth will struggle for answers often taking one step forward only to be thwarted and falling two steps back.

- This is the portion in the story where a ticking clock is introduced or pressure is put on the sleuth to find the culprit before a secondary event happens that makes finding the solution impossible. While this time element isn't an essential element for cozies, it is recommended to keep the story's pacing tight.

- This is also the act where the author should capitalize on the occupation or premise set forth in the beginning. The skills inherent to your sleuth's specialty should be on full display. For example, if your sleuth is a pet whisperer, have dogs or cats helping her dig through a pile of dirty clothes to find the murder weapon. At the end of Act II, i.e. the middle of the story, there should be a turning point with a devastating conflict or reveal that causes the story to pivot in a new direction and forces the sleuth to leave her comfort zone and redouble her efforts to find the truth. This could be a second body, the loss of evidence, death of a key witness, or the clearing of a chief suspect.

[1]The end of Act II is where you would put a second murder or near-deadly attack on the sleuth. Not only is this motivation for the sleuth to act more urgently and efficiently but also a sign that what the protagonist is currently doing isn't working. You're welcome to make this second death predate the first, if such a mode fits your story, but the fact that the main character doesn't find out about it until the novel's midpoint should speak to the fact that the killer still has the advantage. But with that said, a second body only works if the death is a significant

blow to the investigation—such as the person suspected to be the killer dies, someone dies to save the protagonist, or a character dies before he can tell the sleuth the truth. Basically, the second death should bring new problems that cause the sleuth to reevaluate.

Act III: Complications

> **Whittle down suspects via means, motive, opportunity, et cetera**

- The sleuth may need to revisit some characters interviewed in the prior act. She should approach the party armed with new information or better leverage to get the desired answers. If your cozy is on the darker side, the protagonist may now be willing to cross some moral lines or take some risks that she wouldn't or couldn't cross before.

> **Narrow in on killer as violence escalates and the stakes get more personal**

> **Resolve subplots or have them converge with the main plot on the road to resolution**

- Remember, subplots at their most basic level should always intertwine with the main plot and enhance the story's overall conclusion. If they are just hanging out there on their own with no clear connection to the protagonist's motivation for sleuthing or the crime itself, cut the subplot or reevaluate its role in the story.

> **False Lead or Black Moment**

- At the end of Act III, the sleuth should find out that

something she believed all along isn't true. Or better yet, she loses something or someone (third corpse!) valuable, so her faith and everything she believes to be true vanishes. If that's hard, an alternative here would simply be to have the sleuth hold a strong hunch about the identity of the killer but not know how to prove it because she's been using the wrong strategy all along. This leads to an epiphany where the sleuth finally sees something she missed or minimized. She may have to sacrifice something or overcome her internal wound to get this new knowledge. Anything that makes it appear as if the sleuth might fail can work for the "Black Moment." Think of this as the point of no return where the sleuth must solve the crime or die trying (even though we'd never have a cozy protagonist die). If possible, link the epiphany, which really occurs at the top of the fourth act, to the sleuth's wound so the motivation for the showdown in Act IV is connected to the growth the character is due to experience when she successfully solves the crime.

Act IV: Climax and Resolution

> **Confront the key suspect**

- This key suspect may or may not be the actual killer, depending on how you plot the end of the previous act, but during this confrontation the truth begins to unfold.

> **Explain howdunit, whydunit, and how the clues connect—ideally with an emotional payoff**

> **Unveil the killer (the showdown)**

- There should be some face-off here between the sleuth and

the killer where your protagonist triumphs. How severe or mild this interaction should be will depend on your preference, and this book covers some tips for this in the section on showdowns.

- As noted in almost every mystery class the world over, the ideal moment for the audience to realize the truth about the killer's identity is the page before (i.e. three or four paragraphs) the sleuth announces the solution. This is a balancing act that all writers grapple with, so don't blame yourself if you fail to achieve this feat on the first try. However, this timing is an essential element to a killer cozy because it beats the sleuth to the punch and allows the audience to feel like they've succeeded in the act of playing along. But at the same time, the two points are close enough together that the reader won't get restless waiting for the sleuth to reach the same conclusion.

> **Restore justice, tie up loose ends, and return to the ordinary life**

- What is considered the "ordinary life" may have changed slightly for better or worse and that's okay. The important thing here is that the ending is upbeat and happy. The good guys won and the bad guys lost for the sake of helping everyone in the community continue with their lives. This is different from other forms of crime fiction where endings can tend to be dark and the line between good and evil is sometimes murky.
- Once the crime is solved, include a wrap-up that details your sleuth's mindset—she should have learned something, gained new insight on a problem or weakness, or experienced an emotional change. Some authors even like to end the story in a similar fashion to which it began to highlight this growth

in the sleuth. Or if you've included some overarching personal aspect about the sleuth's private life that carries on from book to book in the series, revisit those issues here. Then find a way to leave hints or mild cliffhangers about the growing relationships among the secondary and recurring characters that will entice your readers to return for the next installment. As American crime novelist Mickey Spillane once said, "Nobody reads a mystery to get to the middle. They read it to get to the end. If it's a letdown, they won't buy anymore. The first page sells that book. The last page sells your next book."

Showdown and Coda

The showdown between the sleuth and the killer occurs in Act IV. This is where the sleuth demonstrates her knowledge of the crime and uses her special skills (profession) to thwart the villain. Traditionally, the police are not involved until the end of this encounter. So the question becomes, how do you ensure this event occurs without making the sleuth look stupid for running head first into danger sans backup? One way, it is to have your protagonist discover the truth at a moment when she is involuntarily or unknowingly left alone with the antagonist so that it is too late to run or hide. Her only recourse is to fight or talk her way to victory. Or perhaps, the antagonist goes to the sleuth to incriminate someone else. And in so doing, the truth is revealed, and our heroine makes her stand. Another possibility is that the killer holds a loved one hostage to lure the protagonist away from safety—such a scenario provides leverage strong enough to send your sleuth into danger. The point is to be smart about how the meetup occurs, especially when you're forcing your protagonist to face her greatest fears.

Showdowns can be a battle of the brains where the sleuth outwits the murderer or a battle of brawn where she outlasts the murderer. Decide by considering the mood and tone of your piece then devise the worst thing that could happen. Remember, this is the climax of the story, so seek to develop maximum excitement, tension, and suspense.

The protagonist will also need to use her professional expertise to both defend herself during this showdown and unveil her knowledge of how and why the crime was done. To be clear, **she must prove to the killer and the audience that her active detection paid off.** Of course, you don't need to give the full explanation. Feel free to save some of this information for the sleuth's personal resolution in the final chapter when the ordinary world has been restored. This will help the manuscript avoid the Scooby Doo effect where the killer stops killing just long enough to confess everything.

Finally, dig into the emotional reactions generated in the showdown. Don't rush the final confrontation. Let the audience experience the sleuth's fear with all five senses. This doesn't mean the pace should be slow. Rather, focus on creating a vivid picture full of sensory detail. To do this, use powerful verbs and figurative language, but keep the sentences short so that the reader's eyes can move quickly across the page, creating the illusion that he or she is moving rapidly toward a conclusion.

Grow Tip: Act IV

As stated at the start of the section, there are many variations in plot structure based on genre and personal preference. But with that said, you may still wonder why I suggest a four-act structure for the modern cozy rather than a three-act structure. In truth, most full-length genre fiction could be divided into four parts. The fact is that second act of most fiction can often be split into two sections with an A-arc and a B-arc. To avoid the confusion that comes with making a distinction between those two sets of rising action, this book counts each arc and section of the overall story as its own act. Hence, the four-part structure where every act ends with a turning point that propels the reader into the next section. This format also gives the sleuth an opportunity to have a three-phase Try-Fail Cycle for her detection efforts, which we talk about in the detection section.

Remember, cozies are all about the restoration of justice so that final moment has to feel...well, justified in order to meet reader expectations. By using four full acts to ramp up the danger, you capitalize on the audience's desire for things to change. Work to have 10 to 30 scenes per act and 40 to 120 scenes overall.

Subplots

These secondary plots should support and eventually interweave with the main plot. If the overall story can sustain without the subplot, then that additional storyline isn't necessary. Strong secondary plots should echo the novel's theme, aid in the sleuth's personal growth, and/or provide insight into the resolution of the crime in some unforeseen manner.

The easiest way to create a mystery subplot is to include the other aspects of the sleuth's life that occur outside her pursuit of the killer. Is she facing a personal crisis at work? Has a family member fallen ill? Is she preparing for a competition? Does she have a crush on the Main Street crossing guard?

Then determine how will those events enhance or complicate the overarching story question of whodunit and why. Find where the plots overlap and build on those connections so the two storylines feel like a cohesive whole. For example, perhaps her crossing guard crush is discovered to be a key witness, then as their relationship blossoms, he becomes a suspect adding a complication to that storyline.

A Final Word on Plotting

All commercial fiction, but mysteries especially, should invoke the concept of rising action. This is the portion of the plot where the matters introduced at the beginning meet complications and the stakes grow in magnitude with each mounting problem. This means that the killer, although still unknown, continues to kill and the sleuth decides to take greater risks because the crime has become more personal.

The term "rising action" is common throughout fiction and is most notably drawn from the work of German scholar Gustav Freytag, who referred to the typical plot structure as a pyramid:

Freytag's Pyramid

Rising Action

CLIMAX

Falling Action

Exposition

Denouement

Inciting Incident

Resolution

Freytag's vision for story structure doesn't go into the depth we need for the mystery genre, but he does cover the basics you'll want to understand before moving forward.

Exposition[1]: Introduces the who, what, where, when, and why of the story as well as any background information we'll need to understand about the story to come. Consider this the story's setup. The exposition should also foreshadow, or hint at the source of a potential conflict that has yet to come to the main character's attention.

[1] In recent years, the word "exposition" has taken on a negative connotation and has erroneously become synonymous with "info dump-

ing," which is a glut of unmotivated backstory that bogs down the manuscript. Avoid this tendency in your work by ensuring that each use of backstory has an identifiable purpose and refrain from letting backstory do the work of action, dialogue, and conflict.

Rising Action: This is where the story's complications begin and is noted by the inciting incident, which is an event that destabilizes the ordinary world and introduces the conflict on which the story will be built. The action should continue to rise throughout the story, so the author must introduce new complications throughout—ideally near the end of each act.

Climax (or Turning Point): This moment has great emotional intensity. While long-form fiction will have one major climax near the end of the book where the plot's outcome and the character's fates are revealed, there should also be several mini climaxes known as turning points at the end of the first three acts. These moments revolve around a crisis, which is the instance when a conflict peaks and the protagonist must make a decision. This decision should then lead to a discovery, disaster, or epiphany—depending on sleuth's proximity to the final solution. But regardless of whether it's a mini or a major climax, the moment must involve some internal change in the protagonist that prompts further action. There are several names for these mini-climaxes—turning points, plot points, pivot points, pinch points—and you story can have more than the three mentioned for the end of each act (it's just that those are mandatory). These turning points and the major climax should do one or more of the following when they unfold:

> Raise the stakes so that it becomes impossible for the sleuth to turn back or for life to return to normal until the crime is solved

> Shift blame among the suspects

> Alter the sleuth's understanding of the crime

Think long and hard about these elements and discard anything that feels predictable. You always want to be one step ahead of your audience, so work to give them the unexpected.

Falling Action: This is the story's emotional release or the de-escalation of tension as the story cruises to its conclusion. The audience should also feel a moment of catharsis where they release any emotions or fears built up during the climax.

Conclusion or Resolution: Best defined as the moment of closure when the conflicts have been resolved and the storylines have stabilized; also known as the denouement. Some novels may also include an epilogue which goes the extra step of advancing to a significant time period into the future to reinforce the theme and provide insight into the characters' lives since the resolution of the conflict.

As mystery writers, we want to take Freytag's five basic elements and look at them in terms of a longer period of rising action and a shorter period of falling action. The exposition in this case is the establishment of the ordinary world, the introduction of any background that prepares us for the mystery, and the inciting incident. The climax remains the story's major turning point and includes the Black Moment (and eventual epiphany) leading into it and the showdown leading out of it. The denouement is still the resolution and coda (or epilogue).

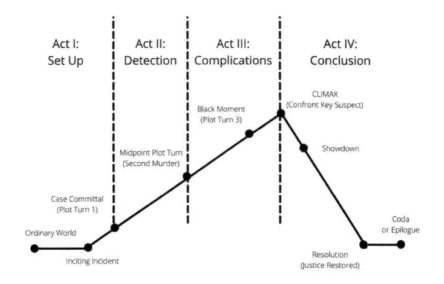

Recap: Plot Structure

ACT I	ACT II	ACT III	ACT IV
Intro. sleuth Intro. victim & criminal Intro. who finds body Disaster leads sleuth to detect	Develop suspects & interrogate Establish clues Intro. sub-plots: e.g. Love interests Evasion or flight by suspects	Eliminate suspects Zero in on criminal Resolve subplots False lead or black moment	Confrontation of criminal Explain clues & connect loose ends Reveal Murderer Restore Justice

PLOT TWISTS

Even though plot twists aren't as closely associated with the cozy mystery genre as they are with thrillers or other forms of commercial fiction, the audience still expects our storylines to deviate from the straight and narrow path of predictability. As you approach the end of your novel, particularly at the end of the third act where the narrative builds to its climax, consider including a major plot twist.

A plot twist is a significant shift in the audience's perception of the story's conflict, specifically how the reader understands the external (plot action), internal (emotion), and philosophical (theme) conflicts that work together to form the narrative. To put it plainly, a good plot twist subverts audience expectations on all levels—physically, emotionally, and thematically—and the main character's entire worldview changes. Two oft cited but incredibly pertinent examples are the "dead people" twist at the end of M. Night Shyamalan's *The Sixth Sense* and the end of *Planet of the Apes* when Charlton Heston discovers he's actually on Earth.

Now, you may be asking yourself how a plot twist differs from a turning point. Well, they're not all that different except that a plot twist is designed to shock and disrupt the audience's belief system as much as the sleuth's. Thus, twisting what we thought we understood into something else completely. Whereas a plot turn is simply a revelatory moment for the main character and may even be foreshadowed enough that an observant reader will see the turn coming even if the protagonist doesn't. Turning points are less about stunning the audience and more about character development, i.e. putting the protagonist in a new situation or forcing them to face a new problem.

But with that said, why should a writer include a plot twist in her story? What is the point? Why are such twists important?

Plot twists are useful because they keep the audience engaged and leave a memorable mark on the reader. For fiction to feel relevant to the audience, the narrative's events, emotions, and themes should reflect the shifts in life we all go through.

To start developing a plot twist, consider a high-impact life event that could cause your protagonist to question her beliefs about her current reality. For example, the death of a loved one could cause your heroine to start digging into her past where she unearths a life-shattering family secret. So perhaps another simple way to develop a plot twist is to consider, how the twist will alter the protagonist's belief system, behaviors, and emotions.

You can also create a plot twist by providing new evidence that will cause the audience to shift their assumptions about where the plot is heading for the duration. For example, hidden murder motives are an excellent way to develop a plot twist, and you can build them by assigning someone an unexpected motive or by subverting the most commonly used motives. For example, the lecherous gardener seen lurking around the victim's house could turn out to be undercover cop who eventually saves the protagonist's life when the killer gets too close.

Below, you will find some common mystery plot twists your sleuth can encounter during the course of her investigation.

> An ally of the protagonist is found to be the villain

> A major belief is discovered to be a red herring or false lead

> A resolved conflict produces a new unforeseen snag that requires resolution before the protagonist can move forward

> A new piece of information reveals the story has an unreliable witness or suspect

> A new character appears or an old one thought to have died returns to provide new information about the mystery

> An important character dies early in the narrative

> A minor character is proven to hold a much more significant role in the narrative than previously understood

Of course, you can create your own plot twists, but make sure they have taken root in the story you've already established. That is to say, you've setup all the elements that justify the shift when it occurs so the audience can look back and see the logic in the change, and you've given the twist a significant series of consequences that alter the physical, emotional, and intellectual/thematic stakes for the protagonist, which will help the audience know how to react to this shift. After all, if the audience is confused, they cannot have a clear emotional reaction, which means your plot twist—no matter how earth-shattering—will have no real effect on the reader.

DETECTION

Taking the Reigns from the Police

Killers in cozies always have a cover story because the structure requires the murderer's identity be concealed until the sleuth sifts out all of the clues for the end reveal. Because the killer blames others and acts covertly, many cozies begin with a death. The tough part for writers is how to get the amateur sleuth, someone who usually isn't correlated with law enforcement, involved in the case. Since the first-act focus for a cozy mystery is to prove that there's an intentional murder, start by placing one strong quantifiable clue (that the cops have overlooked or disregarded) in the protagonist's hands early in the story. Or ask yourself: What's odd about the murder that attracts the sleuth's attention?

Solid answers here will help justify the heroine's sudden mistrust of the police and fuels the story question of whodunnit. Consider why and in what manner the police fail to do their duty. Then determine what event or circumstance could pull your sleuth into the action and send the police off course, allowing your sleuth to take over. You'll also need to find ways to connect the crime to the sleuth's job—or at least highlight the ways her skills as a knitter, baker, or interior designer will help to solve the crime. Here are a few scenarios to consider, but you can always find your path:

> **Scenario #1:** The police refuse to classify the crime as murder because they believe the death is accidental or a suicide and therefore does not require an investigation of outside suspects. This forces the protagonist to step forward on her own to seek the truth.

> **Scenario #2:** Law enforcement refuses to investigate at all because they believe the crime is outside their jurisdiction and must be handled on the state or federal level, giving the protagonist reason to seek the answers for the sake of her community.

> **Scenario #3:** The cops have arrested or are considering the wrong suspect. In this instance, it is particularly imperative that the main character has that strong clue we discussed, which leads her to believe law enforcement has let the real murderer walk free. She then takes the law into her own hands.

Be advised, since cozies focus on an amateur sleuth who in real life would never be able to get themselves near a crime scene, we also need to make sure the sleuth also has a personal connection to the crime—i.e. she knows the victim or gets accused herself wherein her goal would be to prove she's been framed, whodunit, and why. Of course, the audience will have to engage in some suspension of disbelief that a baker or knitter would undertake the daunting task of hunting down a killer. Luckily, that bit of good will is inherent to the genre as long as the author holds up her end of the bargain by illustrating how the police failed to meet their duty.

Of course, you are still allowed to have the police help the protagonist if, say, she is dating the Deputy Chief or is sister to the first female Sheriff, but be creative and subtle with the law enforcement help your main character is given. We want her to do the work and be the star character the audience falls in love with. That's how a single cozy quickly becomes a bestselling series.

Here are some additional reasons you can add to your plot as further motivation for the sleuth to get involved in the crime:

> The sleuth has a special area of expertise or inside knowledge the police don't have.

> The crime parallels one that happened to the sleuth in her youth, so she identifies with the victim or the accused (who she believes is innocent) because of that past trauma.

> The sleuth has reason to believe she's next on the killer's hit list.

As you can see from both the plot points and the supplementary scenarios for the amateur's involvement, you must build a connection between the sleuth and a significant element of the crime. This will act as an incentive for the sleuth when things get dark and become the fuel that drives her action forward as the story unfolds.

Your next job will be to do some brainstorming about the detection section of the book. This means going back to the three or five people who want your victim dead and coming up with ways for your sleuth to confront them once she decides to take the case. Will she question them directly or seek the counsel of their spouses or coworkers? Will her investigation be known to those around her and will she seek their aid, or will she work covertly under the cloak of night sneaking into suspect's homes or offices? Try to create moments that will capitalize on your sleuth's professional skills as well as attack her personal weakness. And if you know there are certain elements you'd like to stand as clues, begin to look for multiple explanations that can tie one or all of your suspects to those ideas. This will give your sleuth several investigative paths to follow and create a twisty puzzle for your audience to unravel.

Deductive Reasoning

In a cozy, the amateur sleuth must have proactive investigative tactics even though she lacks the authority and resources that come with law enforcement. This involves questioning neighbors, uncovering clues, and analyzing information. Detection happens primarily in the middle of the book during the second and third acts. To make your sleuth look as smart and as active as possible, avoid too much of the following:

> Overhearing
> Entertaining false confessions
> Wild speculation
> Hunches
> Coincidences and accidentally run-ins
> Using luck to find clues
> Unfounded connections

When you rely solely on these tactics rather than using real clues or evidence as discussed earlier, you're allowing the sleuth to base her theories on hasty guesses and untested information. Many of the items on this list are either subjective in their interpretation or based on sweeping generalizations, so the reader knows there is error involved in the logic. Thus, they don't trust the tactic because any number of random theories can be drawn from such a shaky foundation. Basically, if a reader doesn't trust an aspect of your story, you're doomed.

Gut feelings should never resolve a mystery. The resolution should come from the sleuth's investigative prowess.

Instead, strive for strong deductive reasoning based on facts established earlier in the story—perhaps ones developed prior to the crime—so that the reader can follow along with your protagonist's logic. Once a story element or clue, such as a suspect's baseline behavior, is established as true, the reader can be more confident that the conclusion drawn is also true. In other words, extrapolation on a central idea works best if your characters are basing their deductions on concrete evidence like surveillance video, fingerprints, bank records, scheduled deliveries, town history, et cetera.

Creating Killer Q&A

The bread and butter of a cozy mystery is having your sleuth canvass the community for information about the crime. This means a number of scenes where your main character will have to ask questions and gather enough information to move the story forward. Unfortunately, this interrogative method of character interaction runs the risk of becoming repetitive, so here are a few things to keep in mind when drafting those scenes.

> **Worldbuilding.** Most of the suspects in a cozy are going to be friends, neighbors, and family, so your initial reaction as a writer may be to have your sleuth simply travel from home to home. However, this limits your opportunity to build the community that will make your series unique. Strive to show off your chosen locale. Corner your suspects for questioning at the local diner or find them down by the wharf where the rich teenagers in your town practice crew. Look for opportunities to make your setting as colorful as your characters.

> **Create tough suspects.** Just because your sleuth will often be dealing with people she knows, doesn't mean every conversation must unfold without conflict. All of your suspects should have a secret they are reluctant to share, so the sleuth has to work to gain the answers she seeks—even if that means going back to that character for a second time later in the story. Have your sleuth exercise her manipulation and cunning against her chosen investigative target. If it helps, think of the interaction as a mental game of chess. Ask yourself, which secrets will the suspect reveal and when? Thinking of the scene this way avoids the predictability of having every interaction be a blubbering admission of guilt.

> **Provide confrontation.** This is a logical progression of the above suggestion. Sometimes things get heated. Don't be afraid to add stakes to the interrogation by adding the danger of someone getting hurt via a cut, slap, or punch. Remember, not every suspect is going to be great at concealing their intention (means, motive, opportunity, or alibi) by using words alone. Some may even try to turn the tables and be the one asking the sleuth tough questions.

> **Falsehoods.** Some suspects will lie because they can't tell the truth due to a coverup for someone else or because they have a secret that makes them look guilty or corrupt. Just remember, a character must have a specific reason for their lie—even if that falsehood is a lie of omission. Suspects who lie are fun because they give the sleuth a challenge and hint at a specific place where she should dig deeper.

> **Create dodgy suspects.** The dichotomy of a chatty witness who suddenly dodges or balks at a certain question or topic can be an easy way to raise the stakes and hint at the direction in which the sleuth needs to dig. Or better yet, one disgruntled suspect may implicate another, sending the sleuth back to square one or providing the sleuth two opposing theories with which to grapple.

> **Cut to the chase.** Eliminate all the mundane junk that happens before and after the scene (hellos, goodbyes, travel, et cetera) by having strong transitions that denote the passage of time or the movement of characters. We want to keep the story moving at a brisk pace and avoid anything that doesn't advance the mystery. This doesn't mean you should never have a point in your story where the sleuth goes over the clues with a partner. It simply means that those scenes

should occur with intention at specific intervals and should be devised to inform the audience of the sleuth's theories, what she's learned from each suspect, and what she hopes to learn from the next one.

The interrogation of suspects will encompass the bulk of any cozy mystery manuscript, so make each interaction as interesting as possible.

The Try-Fail Cycle

One the most cherished teachers in my graduate program, Author Timons Esaias, taught a class on scene building that introduced the try-fail cycle. This basically means that for your story to evolve, you must be cruel to the protagonist by having them make multiple attempts before achieving success. This try-fail cycle as it pertains to the mystery genre is tied to the act of detection and occurs during the second and third acts. If it helps to think of this try-fail-detect combo as a three-phase process, here is what that would look like:

> Phase I: Sleuth works to identify suspects, thus establishing the problem and its difficulty

> Phase II: Sleuth discovers the problem is too big to be solved with a single solution

> Phase III: Sleuth realizes the truth and is drawn into danger

To be clear, if a writer thinks of detection as a process that unfolds in three phases, that's not an indicator that the sleuth needs to visit or question every suspect three times. This just means that once the suspects are established, the main character needs to take at least three proactive stabs at finding the solution.

The Try-Fail Cycle starts in Act II and runs through to the end of Act III. This means that the stakes inch upward each time the sleuth takes a swing at the solution. Each attempt should make the sleuth more frustrated and desperate for answers, or I should say, willing to take risks she wouldn't normally take in an effort to finally get something right. This does not mean you need to describe your sleuth as being physically pathetic, sweaty, frantic, or paranoid, but she should be proactive and working so hard that no stone or potential solution goes unanalyzed.

Remember, the first act is your setup, the second act is detection, the third act is a complication in the detection, and the fourth act is your climax and resolution. So let's talk about how the three phases, heretofore known as the try-fail-detect combo, fit into that plot structure.

So during your second act (i.e. phase one of detection), the interrogations are simpler because the sleuth is still gaging the magnitude of the problem. Early suspect interviews may go poorly simply because she doesn't understand the difficulty or gravity of the situation. And if she does unearth clues, she may not be able to interpret them properly because she hasn't gathered sufficient information.

As the suspect list narrows in act three (i.e. phase two of detection), the sleuth may pinpoint one or two suspects to revisit and gather new clues to examine. A secondary evaluation of her gathered information presents a murky picture of what may have really happened at the time of the murder. The sleuth begins to formulate a plan for resolution, but the simple answers she hopes to find are nowhere in sight—for every right answer, there are two wrong ones.

In the last couple of scenes in act three (i.e. phase three of detection), one suspect arises above all others and the appearance of success is in the sleuth's grasp. However, as the act ends, the sleuth runs into one last major obstacle, usually one that turns everything the sleuth has learned on its head. Of course, the sleuth now has all the tools and information they need to overcome this setback and expose the truth, they just don't realize it. It's this last dark element of unknowing in the trial-fail-detect combo that pushes us into the climax that must occur in act four. Once the sleuth sorts out her blind spot and comes to the realization that she has the right answer (or that she has the proof she needs), she'll have exactly the mental wherewithal to improvise effectively when faced with the killer.

Analyzing Evidence

The pacing in many cozy mysteries runs the risk of grinding to a halt because there inevitably comes a moment when the main character must sit down with a cup of tea and sort through the evidence to determine what she's learned. Even if your character doesn't drink tea, she will need to mull over what is and isn't working about her investigation. So the question becomes, how do we make the act of analyzing information physically active enough that it will be engaging for the audience to read?

The easiest way to do this is to add a sleuthing partner, secret source, or confidant with whom to share ideas. If you're an old timer think about the Scooby Doo gang's dynamics, slightly younger folks may draw a better example from *Veronica Mars* where Wallace and Mac supplied administrative and technical aid to the titular character. The point is that your sleuth should have a mastermind group or at least one person they can use as a sounding board. Ideally, this partner in crime should have specialty knowledge in an area your sleuth lacks. That way, the secondary character complements your main character, allowing the two parts to come together to make a greater whole.

The additional benefit of having your sleuth's partner be an expert in another area allows them to do some sleuthing on their own and/or opens the door for the sleuth to enter settings that she wouldn't otherwise be able to enter. This is why you see many cozy mystery protagonists have a law enforcement love interest or a best friend with medical expertise. The juxtaposition of occupations, or even social classes if you so choose, allows for a wider net to be cast during the detection portion of the story.

Once the team starts analyzing evidence, they can test their theories and beliefs by making maps, reviewing surveillance video, creating timelines, or even reenacting the scene. The possibilities are endless! Just remember, when examining the details of a crime, the sleuth must be one step ahead of the reader. If the audience can think of it, the sleuth must think of it first so that she doesn't appear naïve and so the overall story maintains credibility. We are already stretching the realms of realism when we have an interior decorator or a caterer solving crimes, so we want to be as realistic and capable as possible when it comes to the conclusions drawn. In this respect, it may help to intersperse these brainstorming sessions throughout the three-part try-fail-detect combo, which will force the sleuth to reconsider her position during each phase as she learns something new or her perspective changes.

So now that our protagonist has all her evidence in hand, let's talk about that showdown between the sleuth and the slime bag.

The Showdown or Climax (Confronting the Killer)

Thanks to our plot twist driven, TV-loving society, there's an expectation that our amateur sleuth will have a drama-filled showdown with the killer. Gone are the days of Hercule Poirot when the final face-off was simply a matter of gathering everyone into the drawing room and pointing out each person's motive until the guilty party jumped from their seat holding the smoking gun. Today's cozy writers must create endings that are not only more dynamic but less predictable than the days of old.

One way to accomplish this is with dual solution. This is an ending where the sleuth solves the crime and unmasks the perpetrator only to discover a secondary motive and an additional culprit. We see this all the time in horror movies like *Scream*, but it can also be used to great effect in mystery novels as long as the second killer's involvement has been sufficiently indicated throughout the earlier story. The benefit of this particular ending is that it provides a twisty puzzle for the audience. The downside is that you, dear writer, will have to keep track of the off-stage activities of two suspects as well as provide plausible means and motives. That's a lot of work, so be sure you're up to the task.

In my Victoria Justice Mystery series, I take a more straightforward approach. The endings involve the heroine coming to her realizations at the last minute, once she's in the middle of danger, and having to wrest a weapon away from the killer. I do this because she's young and my legal setting makes an action-oriented ending feel warranted. So to ensure my sleuth's victory, I always make sure she has help or has been provided a sufficient weapon for the fight and that she's matched against someone it would be possible for her to overtake.

If you'd like to build an action-oriented ending, consider placing that showdown in a location that is dangerous for the sleuth and has clear advantages for the killer. Even though you as the writer may have prepared your sleuth in the ways I describe above, the reader must feel like the scales are tipped heavily in the killer's favor. To do this, you must initially let your protagonist's big confrontation plan fall apart. If she brings a cop to help make the arrest, have the murderer kill him. If she's afraid of the dark, have the bad guy cut the power. In other words, put your main character in the worst possible position. This sudden peril creates the tension and suspense expected during a super-contentious showdown. Plus, this last-minute element of *will she or won't she succeed* keeps your readers on their toes and raises the stakes in a manner that will make your writing more dynamic.

However, if you don't feel comfortable writing action or have created an older sleuth who wouldn't feel believable engaging in a physical altercation, consider crafting a peaceful or one-sided showdown that's about getting the killer to confess in a public way and having him learn to live with that shame (or deal with dire consequences). For example, the sleuth could decide to stand up at the culprit's family reunion and reveal that he killed his wife's sister during their passionate love affair. How does the killer react? What does he do? Does he run, shoot up the place, or blame someone else?

In this instance, the sleuth may never need to fight with the killer because the wife's family could grab the guy and enact their own vigilante justice. Their reaction becomes the showdown. Plus, since the shock or calamity of the big reveal comes in a public forum where there are grave stakes, the whodunit and whydunit are heightened. This allows the fallout from those two answers to drastically alter the shape of the community moving forward. As an example, check out *Murder, She Wrote* as nearly episode uses this approach since Jessica Fletcher is more matronly than most.

However, don't let your desire for a more peaceful showdown lead you to believe it is okay to skip this plot point altogether in favor of describing the confrontation via some kind of secondary conversation or retelling after the fact. Your ending must unfold in real time. Anything else is unacceptable. Cozies are all about whodunit and readers want the satisfaction of the sleuth facing off against the killer. That way, we finally get to see both sides of the story side by side—the detective versus the deception artist. Besides, with cozies being community based, the sleuth will have some kind of ties with the killer that will need to be explored so that both the protagonist and the audience can understand how the guilty character was able to successfully hide under the sleuth's nose for so long.

With that said, cozies are still a subgenre steeped in subtly. Even though you want to give the audience something action packed, you don't necessarily need to worry about crafting car chases and shootouts. Instead, focus on designing an emotional ending that resonates with the same wallop as a hard-core punch. Think of cozy conclusions as falling on the scale somewhere between polite society and pandemonium. Amidst the showdown, we want to provide the audience a clear sense of certainty about the killer's identity.

Here is a list of things to <u>absolutely avoid</u> when creating your conclusion:

> **Do not imply that the murder could have been committed by anyone or that the killing was random.** The ending to a cozy is about providing an answer to the puzzle, so you must reveal the specific killer(s) as well as why and how they did it. Do not confuse that old adage of "craft your mystery where everyone looks guilty" as license to have a vague ending. You will alienate your audience this way. This is not the genre for such artsy-fartsy tricks. The audience should be able to look back at the clues provided and clearly understand how the sleuth came to the final resolution.

> **Do not forget to give your killer a backstory that supports his motives.** In cozies, the killer is going to be a member of the community, so it is crucial that you introduce that person early and provide them a sufficient enough characterization that their deceit feels warranted. Unlike other mystery subgenres, we're not allowed to have a bad guy be bad for no reason. And if you're really smart, you'll give us a killer for whom the audience will almost feel sympathetic. Almost. A great example is Batman's Mr. Freeze aka Victor Fries. His motivation for killing and robbing is to obtain enough resources to fuel the research for a cure for his terminally ill wife. His reason for being evil is not just anger or malice but also (and more importantly) love—the univer-

sal element that makes Mr. Freeze equal parts monster and human. Adding a similar balance to your story will make it more believable that a killer could walk among those living in your cozy community.

> **Do not craft a crime your killer couldn't have conducted.** For example, don't make the method of murder manual strangulation if the killer only has one arthritic hand. That set up is possible, but not plausible. Avoid creating a killer and method of murder that isn't credible or believable.

> **Do not base the killer's success or failure on fluke or coincidence.** On the flip side, do not have the sleuth stumble upon the truth in some accidental manner—this includes unearned karma and random acts of God. To rely on any of these tactics, wastes the goodwill the story has earned with the audience. Remember, your novel should provide clues that allow the reader to detect alongside the protagonist, and readers can't intuit a character's luck. Therefore, to base your conclusion on such vagaries, isn't playing fair.

> **Do not allow the killer to get away unscathed.** As stated throughout this book, cozies are about the restoration of justice. The retribution may not need to happen in the courtroom, but it does need to happen for the ordinary world to be restored.

> **Do not provide the final explanation without an emotional connection.** Cozies require the sleuth to connect all of the dots. She should not leave any ambiguities. But as she exposes the truth, unearths the secrets, dispels the lies, and unmasks the killer, she should also explain to the reader why this deceit matters to her and how it is going to ultimate-

ly alter the community at large. This, of course, doesn't always have to be done through external dialogue or even at the direct time of the showdown—it could be done internally or via narrator or as a separate chapter—but it does need to happen before the last sentence unfolds.

> **Do not draft an ending that is to simple or glaringly obvious.** If the ending is too easy, the audience will wonder why it took your sleuth so long to figure things out. Strive to surprise the audience with the unexpected. Nothing is worse than the reader getting ahead of your plot—or worse, the audience concluding that your sleuth is dumb and your book is poorly plotted because they could see the end coming a mile away.

Feel free to write a few additional scenes after the big showdown that provide your sleuth closure and return the community back to normal. Of course, this will be a "new normal" where justice has been restored and life has been altered for better or worse in the wake of the murderer's capture. This is also your opportunity to leave the audience wanting more either by alluding to a new mystery to come or hinting that the resolved threat might resurface in a new way. This will help make your ending memorable and, assuming your text is a series, garner interest in the next book.

Denouement

The portion of the story following the climax is known in literary terms as the denouement, which is French for "the untying." During the denouement, order is restored—i.e. the good are rewarded and the bad are punished. Also, all conflicts should be resolved. Every pending question answered. Each loose end squared off. All secrets revealed and entanglements unraveled. This may be a scene or series of scenes and can be as simple as your sleuth having tea with friends to gossip about everything that happened and clarify details not explained during the showdown. Or it may be as complicated as your sleuth having a series of recovery scenes at the hospital while the police question her about her involvement. Whatever form these scenes take, the idea is that the content provides a clear resolution and sense of finality for the audience.

You may hear some authors refer to this section using the musical term "coda." Why? Well, the tendency in the modern cozy is to put epilogue-like material into the section of the book where the denouement normally lives. That is to say, the denouement is the resolution to the conflict, but an epilogue is how the denouement has affected the characters over an extended period time. Contemporary cozies have mashed those two concepts together to form a hybrid entity often referred to as the "coda." This is really just a final chapter that builds on the conclusion by providing greater insight into the main character's personal life and how that's changed since the murder. And yes, this part of the story may feel different from the main structure due to its lighter tone. Hence, the term "coda." But regardless of how you choose to refer to this portion of your novel, the resolution and the sleuth's reaction to those revelations is an essential part of a cozy that cannot be skipped. Readers expect it.

HOWDUNIT

Howdunits differ from the standard modern cozy because they focus less on *who* committed the crime and more on the means used for the murder (i.e. *how* it was done). In these stories, we may know from the beginning which person is guilty due to some circumstantial evidence, the lack of other viable suspects, or an undeniable motive. Thus, the main story question and suspense hinges on discovering the steps the person used to commit the murder without being seen or how they succeeded in killing even though the conditions surrounding the crime seem impossible.

Playing fair with the audience gets murky in these stories, which is why we primarily talk about cozies in terms of whodunit. However, we can learn a ton about concealment from a good howdunit, so let's look at two cozy-ish examples: Perfect alibi stories and locked room mysteries.

Perfect Alibi Stories

Perfect alibi stories are mysteries where the events of the crime are in reality shifted in time from what is initially perceived so that it appears the proposed killer has neither the means (ability) or opportunity (time) to commit the crime. A perfect alibi can also be an excellent way to conceal the murderer in a cozy.

Here are a few ways to set up a seemingly ironclad alibi for <u>one</u> of your suspects. These suggestions are merely coverups for the killer's deceitful acts, so you will eventually need to describe for the reader how he accomplished being in two places at once. Remember, use only one perfect alibi per novel. Having all your characters claim to have one could prove to be a tedious planning feat for you and overly complicated mess for the audience.

> Establish that a suspect is observed somewhere else at what seems to be the time of the crime.

> Establish a suspect who is physically incapable of committing the crime.

> Establish a suspect who is physically distant from the victim or create a murder that is physically distant from the suspect.

> Establish an ongoing alibi that the killer can briefly abandon to commit the crime and then return to once the murder is complete to confirm the continuity of the alibi.

> Create a set of circumstances that the killer can trigger from afar (or that the killer sets up to initiate automatically after a small delay) that will result in someone's death while also allowing the killer to establish an alibi elsewhere as the mechanism unfolds.

> Create a scenario where the killer has booby trapped an item the victim typically uses, but the killer has done so in such a way that the victim himself abandons or disposes of the item prior to his demise (e.g. a poisoned bottle of water).

Perfect alibis aren't just about making the audience believe that a suspect doesn't have the time or talent to commit the crime, they are also about directing the audience to make false assumptions about what those skills and windows of opportunity ought to be as a way of overlooking the guilty suspect. Simply put, a perfect alibi is another way to introduce a red herring into your story.

Locked Room Mysteries or Impossible Crimes

A locked room is not necessarily a literal locked room, but any area that seemingly no one can access without being seen—e.g. a videotaped hallway, a boat in the middle of a lake, an untouched snowy bank. These mysteries became popular in the mid nineteenth and early twentieth centuries starting with short stories like Irish author J. Sheridan Le Fanu's "A Passage in the Secret History of an Irish Countess" (1838) and American author Edgar Allan Poe's "The Murders in the Rue Morgue" (1841). Some of the popular full-length novels later published include *The Big Bow Mystery* (1892) by Israel Zangwill and *The Mystery of the Yellow Room* (1907) by Gaston Leroux.

Three Common Locked Room Solutions

Even though impossible crime writer extraordinaire John Dickson Carr very famously outlines all of the possible solutions to this particular brand of howdunits in his famous locked room lecture—as delivered by the character of Dr. Gideon Fell in Carr's 1935 book, *The Hollow Man*—I've pulled out the three most plausible scenarios for a contemporary cozy should you choose to incorporate some of these elements into your mystery.

> **Murder happens before the room is locked or after its unlocked.** This works as the crime's solution if a deception such as a false attack or a collective attention grabber is used to misdirect focus, permitting the death to occur before the room is secured or during the reopening of the closed space. This is done in such a way that no one notices the murder didn't actually occur when the "locked room" was sealed.

> **Murderer moves in and out of the locked room without detection.** This one in many ways is the most obvious solu-

tion since it usually involves some kind of duplicate key, doctored surveillance footage, or hidden access that allows the killer to gain entry to the secure space. Because this of this mode's simplicity, you'll need to be doubly clever in obscuring the obvious.

> **Murder where the killer is in the locked room the entire time.** The reader, of course, doesn't realize this because part of the misdirect is that the person is either a) concealed b) has a legitimate reason for being there and is thus excluded from initial suspicion c) isn't a person but a pet or special mechanism designed to do the dastardly deed from within or d) may be the victim himself, placing an attempt on his own life to get someone he despises blamed and arrested for the attack.

A locked room mystery is nothing but the subversion of the audience's core beliefs to the 100th degree. That is to say, to make these stories work, you must first create a social situation where the audience wholeheartedly accepts the concept that the victim was alone in a locked room when he died. This may mean spending a ton of time describing how and why that scenario comes to pass. Then everything introduced thereafter challenges that assumption by introducing doubt about when the victim died, the room's level of locked security, and the certainty that the victim was alone until the murderer is revealed.

STARTING YOUR FIRST DRAFT

Start your first draft by tackling the five main elements of your story: premise, sleuth, victim, suspects, and killer. Work through things in the order listed as you'll have a much easier time with your prewriting. For example, the sleuth is the most important character, the one your audience will hang with the entire book, so it is important that you spend the most time on her and do so first while your energy and enthusiasm are high. Craft the victim next because knowing exactly who that person is and what their standing is in the community will make it much easier to determine who might have wanted them killed and why. Next, look to develop three to five suspects. You can certainly have more (not less!), but this is the sweet spot. Lastly, pick your killer based on the person with the strongest motive who will provide the most shock value. Do some additional character work on this person since a cleverly crafted killer is equally as important as the sleuth in a modern cozy.

Once again, here is an easy breakdown of the things you'll need to brainstorming before tackling the first draft.

> **Form a premise.** Use "imagine" and "what if" to create the basic statement that will act as a roadmap for your story. Start by considering the theme. What point will your story ultimately make? What emotional experience will it deliver? Brainstorm the sleuth's internal and external goals and motivations. Summarize the conflict.

> **Establish word count and point of view.** Decide if this is a novel (70K-90K) or novella (45K) and pick a view-

point—ideally, first or third with your sleuth as the POV character.

> **Create a sleuth.** What is her occupation? How does she become involved in the murder investigation? What's at stake for your sleuth once she gets involved?

> **Determine the victim.** What role does this person play in the community? How is the victim discovered, and who makes this discovery? Include the means and mode of death as well as how and when it took place.

> **Brainstorm suspects.** Give each suspect a secret as well as the means, motive, and opportunity to have committed the crime. Determine how these may later become clues.

> **Develop a killer.** Devise a backstory for the killer. What motivated him to commit the crime and why now? Build a timeline of activity for the murderer. Make sure you know what he's plotting, what he's doing, and where he is headed even when he's not on stage because this will be important when unraveling the crime at the conclusion. Create a bread trail of clues: real ones, red herrings, and misinterpretations.

> **Add the secondary and minor characters.** These are the people who will populate your sleuth's personal world and give her the additional skills, knowledge, access, and support to solve the crime.

Once you've completed the above character sketches, go back and layer in the smaller details as it pertains to the typical four-act mystery structure. Use all of your prewriting to develop an outline and draft scene cards.

Organizing the Narrative Using Scene Cards

After you brainstorm, create your character sketches, and devise your outline—but before you begin your first draft—create some scene cards. While drafting cards isn't a necessary step, many writers find them helpful since you can shift the cards around and carry them with you anywhere inspiration strikes. This makes them a powerful tool for your scene writing. Of course, you will still need to develop the story in a manner that correlates with the plot expectations for the genre, creates tension, and raises the stakes as the story progresses to the climactic showdown. So it is imperative that you study the four-act structure outlined in this book. Play with the order of the cards until you have that perfect formula, and start anew with fresh cards if things don't feel right. That's the beauty of the creative process, things don't need to be perfect the first time around.

Here are some elements that should go on the notecards you'll use to plot your scenes. Feel free to add your own touches.

> **Scene Number:** Once you decide the final order of your scenes, give each a number to ensure that you stay on track when you start to write. It is highly recommended that you write the scenes in the same order they'll appear in the book, and having a scene number will prove helpful if you ever drop or misplace your cards.

> **POV:** Note the scene's point of view as well as the name of the character who will provide the audience's perspective for the scene. This may not be necessary to do every time if your novel only has one POV and one viewpoint character.

> **Date/Time:** Mysteries are puzzles that rely on a logical sequence of events, so smart writers keep a timeline to ensure that the plot makes sense. Putting this information on your

scene cards will prove helpful when establishing setting, noting descriptive elements like clothing, creating alibis for each character, et cetera.

> **Location:** Try to be as dynamic as possible with the physical settings for each scene. Remember, not every conversation needs to happen at the local dinner. Mix it up!

> **Characters:** Create a list for each scene and ensure they have a reason for being there. Each character should have a goal, motivation, and conflict for that specific point in the story even if he or she isn't the viewpoint character. This will keep you from developing characters who are mere pawns that the protagonist or antagonist use at their whim. Flat characters are a no-no for cozies where personality is king. Readers want to fall in love with the community, not just the main character. Thus, the first thing you should do after establishing your premise is a deep character sketch for all of your key players. Do all of your sketches before starting your outline and creating your scene cards.

> **Action:** List three major events that will occur, and describe the sequence of events that need to happen to propel the story forward.

> **Conflict:** Outline the source or point of conflict for the scene. What does the sleuth want to get out of this situation, and who or what stands in her way? Then describe the dilemma or challenge that ends the scene and spawns the action for the next.

> **Purpose:** How does this scene fit into the manuscript's overall plot? What new questions does this scene raise to

keep the reader interested and the story moving forward? This will come in handy later down the line when editing as you'll quickly be able to discern whether a scene is substance or filler.

> **Miscellaneous:** Leave room on the card for describing an image, line, person, song, or quote that may come in handy as inspiration.

If you live firmly in the 21st century and the idea of using paper notecards feels archaic, try an electronic solution by organizing each scene into a table using Google Sheets or Excel. Another option is to create a virtual corkboard using the online organizational tools at Trello.com[1] where you can sort your electronic notecards with a simple drag and click.

How to Write a Scene

This book has been developed with the assumption that its readers have mastered the basic tenets of storytelling, but there are specific scene writing rules that I'd like to highlight as they cannot be overlooked when crafting a cozy.

First, we want scenes that produce a legitimate change with significant stakes, so it is best to tell your story in real time rather than flashback or epistolary form. Moreover, each scene should involve conflict—even those where the sleuth engages in a simple question and answer with a suspect. In literature, conflict is defined as one character standing in the way of what another wants, so have your sleuth walk into each scene with a specific goal that her scene partner and/or the killer will want to thwart. This adds tension to each scene.

In a mystery, the sleuth's goals are going to be a variation on her desire to uncover the truth, but this should also include certain height-

---

eners such as the sleuth's need to overcome her long-standing fear of heights in order to track the killer. Our task as writers is to explain for each scene why the protagonist wants to achieve her goal and how the information she gathers throughout the story will affect her, the crime, the killer, and the community as well as how all those things advance the plot and raises the stakes.

Of course, her success at getting the information and tools she needs initially fails and requires further investigation. This hard luck road of detection is an inherent part of the Try-Fail Cycle that's embedded into the four-act structure; therefore, the sleuth doesn't see the big picture until the final act and isn't given full verification until the resolution.

If you're a new writer, I recommend doing character sketches and plotting your story in advance via a standard outline. Use the plot structure discussed in this book to create a beat-by-beat picture of your entire mystery from beginning to end. You can then chart each scene on index cards with a light sketch of the basic scene so that you don't sit down each day to a blank slate. Plus, once your index cards are complete, vowing to use two or three per day to write your scenes will keep you on track to finish your novel in a timely fashion.

Since mysteries are based on secrets, lies, complications, and plot turns, every scene must be strong, build on the one before it, include active detection, and provide high stakes throughout. A solid way to determine if your scenes are compelling is to grab your scene cards and **ask yourself the following <u>before</u> writing the scene:**

> In a perfect world, what does my sleuth want to happen?

> What does she go into the scene believing and why? How does that influence what she thinks will happen? (This shouldn't be the same answer as the first question.)

> What is at stake?

> What will it cost my sleuth to get what she wants?

<u>After</u> writing the scene, ask yourself the following:

> Does this scene alter life for one or all of the characters involved? Has my sleuth changed?

> What will each character do as a result of that change?

> Does my sleuth see things differently than when the scene opened? Can she see a way through the growing conflict?

> How will my sleuth adjust her approach moving forward to ensure she gets what she wants for the next scene?

> Is it clear to the audience why the sleuth made the decisions she did and how she'll make her new decisions moving forward?

These questions will ensure that, as you write, you are stacking reaction on top of action and that every cause has an effect. Because mysteries are puzzles, stories must unfold logically with each new discovery building clearly and cohesively toward the conclusion. These questions will help you get there and provide clarity to the audience.

Cozies as a Series

While there are certain guideposts every good cozy mystery should follow, we shouldn't think of them as predictable plug and play concepts where the writer fills in the blanks like a Mad Lib. With each new book, work to introduce new characters, devise new elements of setting, provide additional diversity to the cultural or lore, and vary the types of crime. Subvert the societal norms where possible and bring your own experience to the genre to boost interest.

As you write, keep in mind that cozies reside in a subgenre where sequels are expected. This means that your character development and world building must be clear and focused so that you have a foundation on which to build when your novel gets picked up for publication.

Therefore, consider your overall series arc prior to drafting your first novel to avoid rewriting the same story in future iterations. But at the same time, make sure that each book in your series can act as standalone for those readers who enter mid-stream. If you want specific help with this type of advanced planning, I recommend Sarra Cannon's YouTube channel[2] to learn more about how to plan a series.

2.   https://www.youtube.com/playlist?list=PLg6zjsQP4PwdmQG45bTonDlbIS1NcL-dy

REVISION

Becoming an author is a tough business. Just walk into your local bookstore or public library to understand the vast scope of the arena you're entering. Therefore, it is essential that any writer serious about taking their manuscript to the publication level—be that indie or traditional—should learn as much as possible about the craft of writing and revision to establish a sense of professionalism in their work. There are too many books out there for you to expect that an ill-conceived, grammatically sloppy, or unoriginal manuscript will make the bestseller list. You must work to polish your manuscript prior to releasing it into the wild whether that's by hiring a professional editor to help or learning to put a self-induced shine on your masterpiece.

You should also work your hardest to adhere to submission guidelines and follow directions. If they are looking for a horror flash fiction piece, this is not the time to submit your 45,000-word noir novella. Be mindful of the word limits, formatting instructions, genre stipulations, synopsis requirements, et cetera because agents and acquisition editors will surely use any little misstep as an excuse to move onto the next manuscript in line.

Macro-Editing: Big Picture Ideas

Allow a week or so between the first draft and your initial round of revision so that you can gain some objective distance between yourself and your work. When you return to the manuscript, read each chapter several times. With each pass focus on a different aspect of revision: premise, setting, dialogue, action, pacing, characterization, and mystery structure. Here are some questions to consider that might help you distill those larger concepts into more manageable chunks:

> Does the book have a good hook? Examine the first paragraph as well as the overall premise.

> Have I effectively balanced internal and external dialogue, action, and narration?

> Does the dialogue advance the plot?

> Is the action purposeful? Does it move the story forward? Is it believable?

> Does each scene have a purpose and advance the plot? If not, is there a better agenda or sequence to depict?

> Do the characters stay in character? And is it clear how each character helps the conflict or purpose of each scene?

> Does the protagonist have a clear and complete arc? Does the antagonist's storyline feel properly motivated?

> Are the plot twists believable and supported by the story leading into it?

> Do all subplots resolve by the end of the story?

> Is the pacing on target, or is the story marred by irrelevant details, numerous flashbacks, and bulky backstory?

> Have I built an engaging world for the reader? Do I use strong descriptions that engage all five senses?

> Does each scene or chapter stay in a single point of view?

> Can the reader go back to the beginning and trace every clue the sleuth used to solve the crime or pinpoint every hint that foreshadowed the conclusion? If not, rework the clues.

> Does the detective's unique abilities, expertise, experience, profession, or personality contribute to the solution? If not, rework the investigative action for clarity.

> Is it any good? Does it meet reader expectations while at the same time bringing something new to the genre? Have I honestly done everything to make this manuscript the best it can be?

If you can't answer yes to each question, continue working on the elements that fall short of meeting these fundamental standards. If it helps, take a few days between each pass through the revision process. This will allow your subconscious mind to work on any challenges you're facing and give you a fresh perspective on issues you may have overlooked.

Micro-Editing: Mechanics and Formatting

Micro-editing refers to the smaller issues that can sink your manuscript or save it if corrected in time. Consider issues like concision, repetition, word usage, punctuation, sentence structure, grammar, capitalization, consistency, and spacing. You should also make sure all transitions between paragraphs, scenes, and chapters are smooth and logical. And if you describe a real place or complicated process like how to install a carburetor, do your research and check each step for accuracy.

You can set up your word processing software to help with many of these elements and enlist the help of a fellow writer to critique your work and act as a second set of eyes. Here are a few specific examples of the smaller paragraph or sentence-level issues one should review before submitting a final draft. However, I highly recommend that you also develop your own checklist based on your current strengths and weakness.

> **Concision:** Check construction. Keep sentences succinct. Embrace one of the most popular lessons from William Strunk, Jr., and E.B. White's *The Elements of Style*: "Omit needless words." Avoid using "which," "what," "who," "just," and "that" as filler. For example, "Julia was the type of woman who used sex in order to manipulate people," is not as great as, "Julia used sex to manipulate people."

> **Word Usage:** P.D. James, one of the great crime fiction novelists, once said, "Words are the raw material of our craft. The greater your vocabulary the more effective your writing." Build a solid understanding of what words mean and how definitions differ. For example, "pillage" and "rob" are synonyms in *Webster's Thesaurus for Students*. However, one means "rampaging and raping during times of war" and the other means "taking property by threat of force." See the difference. Don't use the word "pillage" when what you really mean is "rob." Keep it simple.

> **Wishy-Washy Words:** "It was as if..." "It seemed like..." "It felt..." "I heard..." "I saw..." "There was..." "It was like..." "She sort of..." "They kind of..." "He probably..." These are weak ways to start a sentence. They show no sense of commitment. Make the action immediate and definitive. "Bells chimed all around me," is better than "I heard the bells chime."

> **Sacrificing Clarity for Duality:** We are all guilty of this: "As Maria picked up a basket of laundry, she turned to face

Leah." We want to show two actions happening at once, but the sentence structure is wordy. Trust the audience will understand the order of actions. This is clearer: "Maria picked up the laundry basket. She turned to face Leah."

> **Exclamation Points and Italics for Emphasis:** Exaggerated punctuation is a sign of muddled writing. F. Scott Fitzgerald once said, "Cut out all these exclamation points. An exclamation point is like laughing at your own joke." Instead, use strong verbs to convey the desired emotion. Find words that enlighten the senses and infer movement or rhythm. If the words on the page still need this crutch, clarify the action.

> **Excessive Use of Modifiers:** Why use "he said angrily" when "he shouted" is more succinct and just as effective? Rely on strong verbs over adverbs.

> **Unbalanced Cadences**: Use parallel construction when creating lists. Bad: Mike loved running, jumping, and to hop and slide. Better: Mike loved to run, jump, hop, and slide. The key here is that the second sentence relied solely on verbs to establish the list rather than mixing various constructions.

> **Idioms:** Peculiar expressions or clichéd sayings like "fast as a bunny" or "quick as a wink" are tiresome to the reader. Use unique metaphors or similes to create a vivid picture. Divine your own images, and don't rely on obvious shortcuts.

> **Negative Structure:** Structure sentences in the positive when possible. "He's never on time," versus "He's always late." The first borders on being an opinion. The second bor-

ders on being fact. The reader will appreciate the more objective perspective that comes from using the positive phrase.

> **Avoid redundancies**: "Don't you dare," Maria shouted. The meaning of the dialogue implies anger, and we can imagine Maria shouting without the dialogue tag. This is an example of unnecessary repetition. The best way to correct this passage, especially if you want to avoid the added words, is to move the story forward with a beat of action: "Don't you dare." Maria slapped him before he could respond.

> **Winks, Nods, and Smiles**: We want our characters to be active and interesting. Make the effort to go beyond the mundane head shake or raised brow. People ball their fists, clench their teeth, wrinkle their noses, et cetera. This goes back to the idea of finding active verbs. But if this is an overall trouble spot for you, obtain a copy of *The Emotion Thesaurus* by Angela Ackerman & Becca Puglisi.

> **Run-On Sentences:** Once again, Strunk and White's *The Elements of Style* advises, "Avoid a succession of loose sentences." The key here is to master basic punctuation. Obviously, we can use the occasional fragment or run-on sentence for the sake of realism in dialogue; however, it is important for a writer to distinguish a compound sentence from a simple sentence through the use proper punctuation (commas, semicolons). Learn the fundamental rules of writing before attempting to break them.

> **Too Much Inner Dialogue:** At the start of your manuscript, don't let more than a few paragraphs go by without dialogue. You risk losing your audience in a sea of tedium. Michael Moorcock, one of the greatest science fiction writ-

ers of our time says, "If possible, have something going on while you have your characters delivering exposition or philosophizing. This helps retain dramatic tension." Keep your characters active and have them engage with each other. Next to action, external dialogue is the best way to move your story forward and helps to maintain a high level of audience interest. Conversation brings conflict, and conflict is the crux of any story. Don't break up good dialogue with paragraphs of internalization. You risk losing the reader and destroying the flow of the scene. The scene's body language and dialogue—what is being said, how it is being said, why it is being said, and where it is being said—should provide insight into your viewpoint character's thoughts. Leave the internal monologue for when the character has a moment to reflect unencumbered.

> **Recreating accents via text:** "I vant too dreenk yer blood." Nobody wants to read a bunch of nonsense words. If a character has an Aussie dialect, tell us he is from Sydney. Give us a few subtle indicators like, "No worries, mate." Then leave it alone. Less is more. Besides, if you're lucky, the audiobook and film versions will give us the desired accent.

> **Sentence Structure:** One way to write better sentences begins with eliminating "it" and "there" as the opening word. Yes, the word "it" can act as a subject; therefore, using the word "it" to start a sentence is grammatically correct. However, ask yourself, which sentence is stronger? *John ate the cake. It was John who ate the cake. It ate the cake.* The second and third examples add needless words and clarity suffers. The same often happens with "there." Again, which is better? *There's four boys in the kitchen. Four boys are in the kitchen.*

Editing Software

PerfectIt, ProWriterAid, WordRake, PaperRater, Slick Write, and Grammarly are fee-based online programs (or word processor add-ins) that claim to do instantaneous editing. While these programs are helpful, I wouldn't solely rely on them when preparing to submit to a publisher or agent because they only catch basic mechanics. Rarely do such programs do as well as a human editor who can recognize inconsistencies like a character's eye color or motivation changing from chapter to chapter. So get a critique partner or learn to revise and self-edit by taking classes. Also, invest in these guides to learn more about cleaning up your manuscript.

> *Don't Murder Your Mystery* by Chris Roerden
> *Self-editing for Fiction Writers* by Renni Browne
> *Revision and Self-Editing for Publication* by James Scott Bell
> *Story Fix* by Larry Brooks
> *The Writer's Little Helper* by James V. Smith, Jr.

Hiring a Professional

Even if you seek professional help to revise your manuscript, it is imperative that you do your best to correct the basic micro-issues prior to submission. This includes formatting, punctuation, usage, grammar, spelling, et cetera. The cleaner and more legible your work, the more likely the editor will be able to see your manuscript's potential. Do not think of your editor as the cleanup crew hired to fix your mistakes or lazy efforts. Their real job is to help you capitalize on your strengths and minimize your weaknesses. A cleaner manuscript will make this job easier and provide an opportunity for them to address more advance issues that might help you stand out from the competition.

Here are the three main types of editors a writer might hire during their quest to polish a manuscript. Think of them as phases on a spectrum from the initial heavy revision to the light edit. Again, this is not something that's required. But if you do hire someone, these descriptions should help you decide what type of editor you need and what to expect from their services.

Developmental Editors

Choose a developmental editor if you want help revising your big picture issues like plot structure, voice, content, and clarity. Ideally, you'd hire a developmental editor before a copyeditor, who deals the smaller issues of mechanics. A good developmental editor will provide guidance on the overall organization of the work, aid in adjusting tone and point of view, help determine what should be added or removed (particularly with regard to reader or market expectations), resolve redundancies, and refine the overall cohesion of the work. Because this type of edit involves a deep dive into your manuscript, expect developmental editors to charge more than a copyeditor or proofreader.

For your money, you should receive a copy of your manuscript with line notes pinpointing where corrections need to be made as well as a separate letter—sometimes referred to as an editorial assessment—suggesting how to implement the necessary changes. Some editors offer these two parts of the service separately to save writers money, so be sure to ask exactly what you're getting.

Also, be aware that developmental editing is also sometimes called "content editing" or "substantive editing." You may also hear magazine or newspaper industry folk refer to the similar process of shaping an article as "line editing." Regardless, this is the most hands-on of the three processes being discussed.

Copyeditors

This job is technically defined as the act of preparing the text, i.e. the copy, for the typesetter. Of course, in today's world, typesetting is no longer a manual process but rather one that takes place almost instantaneously via conversion software. However, the copyeditor's job remains the same—preparing the manuscript for the next step in the publishing process.

Basically, these editors focus on mechanics (grammar, syntax, diction) and logic rather than content. Although, as with anything, these lines are not hard and fast, and you may find some copyeditors willing to do some developmental work if the price is right. But for the purposes of your search, it is essential to know the difference so that you don't overpay for services you don't need.

A legitimate copyeditor will edit your manuscript using track changes or a similar program, provide you with a clean and edited version, and deliver a style sheet, which is a document outlining all of the tiny details that need to remain consistent throughout the manuscript (e.g. spelling of an abbreviated city name—*Philly v. Phillie*).

Proofreaders

This role wasn't originally an editor in the way we think of them today. Their original role was to review the proof and compare it to the copyedited manuscript, looking for anything that didn't reflect the copyeditor's marks as well as any typos and misspellings that eluded the copyeditor. After the proofreader, the manuscript would then go back to the typesetter for finalization. Typesetting was a costly procedure in past years because the process was done with metal on a press. Thus, changes were only executed beyond the copyeditor's marks if the proofreader found that the error or omission was egregious.

These days, even though we still call them proofs or galleys, the process of making those comparative changes has become infinitely easier thanks to computer technology. For this reason, the proofreader's role has essentially become obsolete and many people have taken to using the terms "proofreader" and "copyeditor" interchangeably. So if you're hiring someone who calls themselves a proofreader, a safe assumption is that they are essentially doing a super light copyedit where the goal is to identify any small typos that may have been overlooked in earlier passes by you, your agent, your critique partners, or a copyeditor. But once again, this role currently lacks a clear definition, so it is doubly important to ask for credentials and service terms from anyone you hire in this regard.

For a list of reputable editors in any of these categories, visit the following websites: Editorial Freelancers Association[1], Book Editing Associates[2], or Reedsy[3]. In addition, your professional writing associations (local and national) should have a database of qualified editors. If the number of choices offered by those resources are too daunting, self-publishing professional Joanna Penn has a list of editors on her website (https://www.thecreativepenn.com/editors/).

Grow Tip: Editing

If you go the traditional publishing route and your work is acquired for sale, you will be assigned a book editor whose role will feel like all three of the aforementioned editor types. That's to be expected since this person's job is to shape your manuscript for publication. This editor is responsible for distributing early versions of your work to the in-house sales and marketing staff to spark support during seasonal sales meetings as well as providing suggestions for how the book can be best positioned in the market. Basically, this person is the main cheerleader for you and your novel behind the scenes at the publishing house, so consider this writer-editor relationship one of the most important ones in

---

1. https://www.the-efa.org/

2. https://www.book-editing.com/

3. https://reedsy.com/

terms of your book's success. Be kind to this person and take their suggestions graciously because their goal is aligned with yours: Creating a bestseller.

AUTHOR'S NOTE

Thank you for reading this book. Please help spread the word.
Write an online customer review.
**Join my mailing list to hear about upcoming Writer Productivity
Series titles, which will cover self-editing, legal thrillers, comedy in
fiction, writing action, and writing faster.**
Follow me on Twitter, Pinterest, and Instagram @ajthenovelist
Mailing List: https://ajthenovelist.com/sign-up/
Website: https://ajthenovelist.com/
Join my Facebook[1] for weekly tips and tricks!
Post a review and recommend me on Bookbub[2].
Join my community on Goodreads[3] and leave a review.

---

1. https://www.facebook.com/AJ-the-Novelist-693083501559738

2. https://www.bookbub.com/profile/andrea-j-johnson

3. https://www.goodreads.com/author/show/19764533.Andrea_J_Johnson

RESOURCES FOR WRITERS

Here are a few membership organizations that provide support for unpublished and published authors in the mystery genre. Male and female cozy writers are welcome to join all of these organizations, which have contests, critique partner matches, craft classes, and much more.

Sisters in Crime:
https://www.sistersincrime.org/
Mystery Writers of America:
https://mysterywriters.org/
International Thriller Writers:
https://thrillerwriters.org/
Kiss of Death:
https://www.rwakissofdeath.org/
Top annual conferences that focus on mystery fiction.
Malice Domestic:
https://www.malicedomestic.org/
Left Coast Crime:
https://www.leftcoastcrime.org/
Bouchercon:
https://www.bouchercon.com/
ThrillerFest:
https://thrillerfest.com/
SleuthFest:
https://sleuthfest.com/
Familiarize yourself with a few of the common resources
for writers interested in publication.
In Reference to Murder:

https://inreferencetomurder.typepad.com/

National Novel Writing Month:

https://nanowrimo.org/

Writers Market:

https://writersmarket.com/

Publishers Lunch:

https://lunch.publishersmarketplace.com/

Publishers Weekly:

https://www.publishersweekly.com/

Self-Publishing:

http://www.selfpublishedauthor.com/home

Association of Authors' Representatives:

http://aaronline.org/

Manuscript Formatting:

https://www.shunn.net/format/story/

GLOSSARY

Act – a unit of analysis for dividing a narrative into sequences; although not marked as with a play, the emotional beats of a commercial fiction novel can be divided into three to five acts

Action – the behavior, gestures, or body language that illustrate a character's feelings and attitudes—this behavior should propel plot, provoke reactions, and build conflict

Alibi – proof of having been elsewhere during the commission of a crime or any circumstance that seemingly prevents someone from having committed a murder

Analogy – an extended simile

Antagonist – a character or element in direct opposition or conflict with the protagonist

Antihero – a central character who is deeply flawed and has a twisted moral compass—e.g. doing the wrong thing for the right reason—but whose tragic flaw becomes her source of potential redemption for herself or others, e.g. Annaliese Keating from ABC's *How to Get Away with Murder*

Archetype – based on a recurring concept in culture such as a symbol or character type and speaks to a universal aspect of the human experience

Background – information about a character

Backstory – action that took place before the current events of the plot; the details of a character's past that occurred before the story's start

Beat – a statement used between lines of dialogue to increase the emotion or tension of a scene, usually includes gestures or thoughts that anchor the speaker to the setting

Beat sheet – a document that identifies the key emotional moments in a narrative and lays out what needs to happen in each act of the story

Beta reader – someone who reads a writer's manuscript prior to publication to confirm the work has met the audience's expectations for the genre

Capers – a subgenre of mystery told from the criminals' point of view that involve a light-hearted crime rather than a murder; see also *heist*

Catharsis – purging of emotion; the post-climax release of tension that refreshes the spirit

Character arc – the character's internal journey during the story and how she transforms (positively or negatively) by the end

Character quirk – a strange or interesting character trait

Character trait – characteristics, behaviors, and attitudes that create a character's personality

Characterization – the act of providing a portrayal or description of a character

Characters – the people who occupy a story

Circumstantial evidence – indirect evidence; evidence inferred from one or more sources

Cliché – a word, expression, or phrase that is predictable or overused

Cliffhanger – a suspenseful situation left unresolved until the next beat, chapter, or novel

Climax – the height of a story's pace, action, and tension prior to the ending; the final conflict where it is decided if the protagonist will win and achieve his goal

Clue – a piece of evidence or information used in crime detection

Coda – the portion of the story that serves to round out, conclude, or summarize the lessons learned in the main tale but may also attempt to serve its own interests by answering or posing a new question about the characters' personal lives—unlike an epilogue, a coda is not marked to indicate its separation from the main story

Conceit – an extended metaphor that compares two unlike things in a congruent and often clever manner

Conflict – problem or predicament; the opposing force or obstacle that keeps a character from getting what they want—often broken down in literature as man v. man, man v. nature, man v. himself and acts as the main struggle for the story

Copyeditor – an editor who checks for issues of mechanics

Corroborating evidence – information that strengthens or confirms already existing evidence

Covert murder – an attempt is made by the murderer to cover-up the death

Cozies – a mystery subgenre known for eschewing explicit violence, sex, and gore in favor of off-stage murders in idyllic settings with coverups, suspense, misdirection, and (most importantly) a feel-good ending where justice is restored; also known as *cosy* or *cozy mystery*

Critique partner – a fellow writer who provides feedback on story structure and content prior to publication

Deceitful murder – an attempt is made by the murderer to make the death look like something else, e.g. an accident, self-defense, act of God, suicide, et cetera

Deductive reasoning – the process of demonstrating that if certain key statements are true, then other statements based on them are also true; following one or more factual statements through to their logical conclusion

Deep point of view – a style of writing that strives to place the reader in the protagonist's mind by removing elements that place a barrier between her and the audience

Denouement – French for "untying"; the post-climax resolution of the plot; an essential solution to the plotted conflict

Description – a narrative explanation of the who, what, where, when, and why conveyed as imagery that is either sensory, emotional, poetic, or data-driven in its output

Developmental editor – content editor; also known as a substantive editor

Deus ex machina – Latin for "a god from a machine," which in the days of ancient Greek and Roman drama referred to an actor or deity statue being lifted over the stage by a crane; a plot device in the form of a person, object, or event that appears suddenly and instantaneously fixes an impossible conflict or problem—can be used comically but contemporary literary critics consider this a contrivance, e.g. the entrance of Fawkes at the end of *Harry Potter and the Chamber of Secrets*

Dialogue – speech or words spoken aloud by characters, signaled via quotation marks; (consider dialogue a clear way to keep the story active in the absence of physical movement as dialogue is one of the keys to conflict)

Dialogue tags – the verb after a line of dialogue that signals who is speaking or how the words are being spoken, e.g. said, exclaimed, shouted, asked, et cetera

Diction – word choice

Direct characterization – when the narrator or other characters explicitly describe what a character is like

Direct evidence – positive evidence; any fact attested to by eyewitnesses or information stated in documents that affirms the genuineness and veracity of the data

Disturbance – an event that foreshadows the upcoming turning point

Dramatic irony – when a gap appears between what the audience knows and what a character believes or expects

e.g. – for example

Epilogue – an optional follow-up section that briefly covers personal events that occur some significant period of time after the story's main question has been resolved and concluded, typically marked to indicate its separation from the main story

Epiphany – a sudden realization or insight into a subject's greater meaning

Exculpatory evidence – information tending to excuse, justify, or absolve the alleged fault or guilt of the defendant

Exposition – the initial phase of the plotting arc meant to establish setting, characters, situation, and potential conflict

External conflict – the struggle between the protagonist and an outside force such as nature, society, or an adversary

Falling action – the point of the story after the climax in which the resolved conflict leads to the conclusion and a catharsis for the audience

Figurative language – a word or phrase that conjures an image in the mind of the reader by creating a change in the usual meaning or order of words and/or by comparing or identifying one thing with another, e.g. similes and metaphors; also known as *figures of speech*

First person – an internal narrator who refers to herself using the pronouns "I" or "me"

Flashback – a break in the present narrative to present something that happened before the start of the story

Flashforward – a break in the narrative structure whereby a scene from the fictional future is inserted into the fictional present or is otherwise dramatized out of chronological order

Flat characters – predictable characters with no dimension or personality, e.g. Kenny from *South Park*

Foil – a character who serves as a contrast to another (usually the protagonist) and is meant to draw attention to the strengths and weakness of both parties; a character meant to put the protagonist's action and choices into context

Foreboding – a prediction of misfortune; the feeling of an ominous mood rising

Foreshadowing – a hint to future events

Foretelling – reflecting or briefly hinting at themes that will be further highlighted over the course of the narrative

Genre – the category in which a story falls; in commercial fiction, this includes mystery, romance, science fiction, fantasy, et cetera

Goal – what each character wants or desires

Heist – a subgenre of mystery similar to a caper where the story is told from the criminals' perspective; however, these stories tend to include violent crimes motivated by revenge

High concept – a story with a unique or innovative premise that hooks the audience and deals with the genre's tropes in unexpected ways

Hook – the concept or opening lines of a novel, designed to grab the reader's attention and induce further reading

Howdunit – the narrative's solution focuses on how the murder occurred

Hyperbole – exaggeration or overstatement

i.e. – that is; in other words

Imagery – the sensory component of description that's often created through figurative language such as similes and metaphors

in medias res – Latin for "in the middle of things"; all fiction should start in progress

Inciting incident – an event that upsets the protagonist's ordinary world and sets her on the journey that will occupy her throughout the narrative; also referred to as the *destabilizing event*

Indirect characterization – when a character's traits are revealed implicitly through her speech, behavior, thoughts, appearance, et cetera

Inductive reasoning – making an inference from a general observation or small sample

Info dump – when a writer reveals a large amount of information or backstory all at once instead of spreading it out

Intangible clues – a piece of legitimate evidence that cannot be physically defined such as the habitual behavior of a suspect or an eye-witness statement

Internal conflict – the protagonist's struggle against himself such as flawed drives, habits, or impulses

Internal dialogue – a character's self-talk or inner monologue; thought

Irony – when a statement or situation is characterized by the significant difference between what's expected versus what actually happens or what's understood versus what's meant; in literature, there are three types of irony: verbal, situational, and dramatic

Legal thriller – a subgenre of mystery where the legal system serves as the backdrop and framework for the narrative, e.g. *Presumed Innocent* by Scott Turow

Locked room mystery – a subgenre of traditional mysteries where the crime unfolds under impossible circumstances such as a murder that occurs in a locked room or a victim found murdered in an untouched patch of snow, e.g. *The Hollow Man* by John Dickson Carr

Logline – a one-sentence summary or description of a narrative, usually a screenplay, designed to hook the listener; a short description of a text's premise; also known as *elevator pitch*

Maid-and-butler dialogue – a conversation where a character relays information to another even though both characters already know; an obvious attempt to inform the audience of something; the author's failure to show rather than tell

Manuscript – the term used to refer to a work in progress or an unpublished novel

Mary Sue – a character, usually female, portrayed unrealistically free of faults or weakness

Means – the ability and resources to commit the crime such as access to the weapon or knowledge about the method of murder

Metaphor – a figure of speech where two unlike things are compared, e.g. "Love is a battlefield."

Macro-editing – working to revise big picture issues; to look at the manuscript with regard to content, clarity, voice, and structure

Micro-editing – working to correct small editing issues of mechanics like concision, repetition, word usage, punctuation, syntax, grammar, capitalization, formatting, and consistency

Milieu – the physical or social setting of the narrative; the overall atmosphere or feel of a story, including the environment, culture, history, geography as well as the mood and tone of the text

Mixed metaphor – when two or more usually incompatible comparisons are tangled together in a manner that's unclear and often unintentionally humorous, e.g. "It's our turn at bat, so let's see this project into the end zone."

Modus operandi – Latin for "mode of operating"; in criminal law, this term refers to a pattern of behavior so distinctive that separate crimes or wrongful conduct are recognized as the work of one person

Monologue – a long uninterrupted speech given by one person—can be internal as thought or spoken aloud as dialogue

Mood – the emotion a scene evokes in the reader

Motif – a recurring symbol, sound, action, idea, or phrase within a literary work meant to strengthen the narrative by adding images and ideas to the theme

Motivation – the things driving a character's desire or goals; drive

Motive – an actionable idea or reason to commit the crime

Narrative – the written events of the story as told by the viewpoint character or narrator

Narrator – the person telling the story

Novel – a written work of 50,000 words or more

Novella – a written work of 45,000 words or less

Omniscient point of view – a third-person point of view where the narrator is all-seeing and all-knowing

Onomatopoeia – a word that approximates the sound it describes, e.g. "buzz"

Opportunity – time to commit the crime unseen; an unencumbered chance to follow through on intention

Overt murder – no attempt is made to make the crime look like anything other than a crime

Pacing – the rate of a story's forward progression

Pantsing – the act of writing a novel "by the seat of your pants" without advanced planning

Perfect alibi stories – mysteries where the events of the crime are in reality shifted in time from what is initially perceived so that it appears the proposed killer does not have the means and opportunity to commit the crime; most often used in howdunits but an overall great way to create a plot twist, e.g. *Salvation of a Saint* by Keigo Higashino

Personification – a figure of speech that endows something non-human with humanlike qualities or abilities, e.g. "Death brushed against me."

Personal wound – an internal struggle or blind spot a character has difficulty overcoming or seeing past

Physical setting – place where the action unfolds; also known as *spatial setting*

Pinch point – a small turning point

Plot – the narrative events that unfold as the protagonist overcomes obstacles to achieve her goal; the five main phases of plot are exposition, rising action, climax, falling action, and resolution (or denouement)

Plot device – any technique in a narrative used to move the action forward; also known as *plot mechanism*

Plot hole – an issue, inconsistency, or contradiction in the plot that makes it illogical or unbelievable

Plot point – a significant event that moves the story forward; see also *turning point*

Plot reveal – the answer to a question, which the writer has prompted the audience to ask earlier in the narrative

Plot twist – an unexpected development that shatters what we thought was true; a story turn designed to drastically disrupt things the audience believes they already know and view the story in a whole new light

Plotting – the act of planning your novel structure in advance; the arrangement of the action

Point of view (POV) – the perspective from which events are viewed and the story is told; the focus and voice of the narrator; also known as *viewpoint*

Point-of-view character – the person whose perspective the reader uses to view the story; also known as *viewpoint character*

Police procedural – a subgenre of mystery that depicts the cops using the tools of their trade to solve crime

Premise – the story's main idea or concept; a short but hooky statement that outlines the plot

Presumptive evidence – information that is considered to be fact until proven otherwise; see also *circumstantial evidence*

Prologue – Latin "spoken before"; the section of a literary work prior to the first chapter meant to provide important background to the main story although the purpose of the information may not prove immediately obvious

Proofreader – someone who reads through the document to make sure the copyeditors' marks and suggestions have been honored

Prose – the ordinary form of spoken or written language without rhyme or meter as distinguished from poetry or verse

Protagonist – the main character

Purple prose – writing that tries too hard to be descriptive and is verbose in doing so; also known as *flowery language*

Red herring – a false lead that throws the reader off track or briefly carries the protagonist away from her goal

Resolution – the narrative's conclusion

Revision – the process of looking at your ideas and finding ways to make them clearer and easier to understand

Rising action – the events of the story leading up to the climax

Scene – an event that takes place in a single setting in a set amount of time—a novel is made up of several scenes divided into acts

Second person – a narrator who refers to herself using the pronoun "you"

Secondary character – a person who is part of a subplot or central storyline but does not play as large a role as the main characters

Setting – the time and place where each scene occurs; the unifying element of a story, which ties time, location, culture, mood, tone, characterization, and theme into one milieu

Simile – a figure of speech that makes a direct comparison using the words "like" or "as," e.g. "She's as cute as a button."

Situation – the basic events depicted in a literary work (i.e. what happens); different from conflict in that this refers to the overall circumstances and may or may not involve a struggle or problem

Situational irony – when a character has an expectation that undergoes an unexpected reversal or is fulfilled in an unexpected manner

Stakes – the consequences or reward for the protagonist's success or failure to reach her goal; the character's emotional connection to success or failure

Stereotype – an undeveloped character whose traits stem from a widely perceived misconception associated with them

Stream of consciousness – free association; a narrative technique commonly attributed to the Modernist Era (1900-1940) where a narrator's internal monologue is written to mimic real-time thought patterns and emotions, e.g. *Mrs. Dalloway* by Virginia Woolf

Style – an author's distinctive manner of expression through his diction and imagery

Style sheet – a file that defines the layout and other items of consistency for a large document

Subgenre – a smaller category within a genre

Subplot – the secondary plot in a work of fiction

Substantive editor – content editing; see also *developmental editor*

Subtext – the underlying, implicit, or metaphorical meaning of a dialogue or text; an idea hinted at but not plainly expressed

Subvert – when your words, action, or approach criticize, undermine or overturn the usual way of doing or thinking about something

Suspense – elements that induce the audience state of feeling excited, anxious, or uncertain about what might happen; the purpose is to make the reader more concerned about the characters and form a sympathetic association

Suspension of disbelief – the willingness of the reader to set aside their judgement and accept the story being told; a term most often used with cozy mysteries since their storylines hinge on an amateur sleuth rather than law enforcement solving the crime

Symbol – an image, concept, person, or thing that stands for something else

Synopsis – a summary of the novel's events, including its ending

Syntax – the way words and phrases are put together to form sentences; word order

Tagline – a clever slogan or statement used to market a product, not to be confused with *logline*

Tangible clues – a piece of evidence or information that points to where a suspect has been, i.e. things you can taste, smell, hear, touch, see, or analyze such as fibers and fingerprints

Temporal setting – story time or the current reality for the characters; same as *plot time*

Tension – the potential for conflict or the reader's anticipation of conflict rising

Theme – what your story is trying to say or prove about its topic

Third person – an external narrator who refers to the action using the pronouns "he," "she," or "they"

Thriller – a subgenre of mystery that focuses on a high degree of suspense, adventure, and intrigue to fuel the narrative

Tone – the attitude the work takes toward the material; in fiction, this often reflects the protagonist's attitude toward the story situation

Tragedy – a genre of storytelling where the protagonist is undone (often a fall from greatness) by his own flaws such as avarice, hubris, or jealousy, e.g. *Citizen Kane*

Tragic flaw – the trait that brings the downfall of the protagonist in a tragedy

Tragic hero – a protagonist whose traits earn him sympathy from the audience, but whose flaws ultimately lead to his downfall, e.g. Willy Loman in *Death of a Salesman*

Trope – the storytelling conventions common to different genres

Turning point – an unexpected event, person, or piece of information that raises the stakes and sets the protagonist on a new path; the three moments of action and/or decision that leads from Act I into Act II, Act II into Act III, and Act III into Act IV in a commercial fiction novel

Unreliable narrator – a storyteller who lies, misleads, or withholds information from the reader, either intentionally or unintentionally, casting doubt on the narrative

Verbal irony – when a word or expression takes on a different meaning (usually opposite) than its surface meaning

Voice – the narrator or author's emotions, attitude, tone, and point of view as expressed through diction

Whodunit – the narrative's solution focuses on who committed the murder

Whydunit – the narrative's solution focuses on the motive for the murder

World building – the act of infusing the setting with specific details about the culture, government, geography, politics, religion, etc.

Printed in Great Britain
by Amazon

80475697R00105